START WITH THE ART

START WITH THE ART

THE SMART WAY TO DECORATE
ANY ROOM ON ANY BUDGET

NATALIE PAPIER

and Stephanie Sisco

VORACIOUS
LITTLE, BROWN AND COMPANY
New York Boston London

Voracious / Little, Brown and Company
Hachette Book Group
1290 Avenue of the Americas, New York, NY 10104
voraciousbooks.com

First Edition: October 2024

Voracious is an imprint of Little, Brown and Company, a division of Hachette Book Group, Inc. The Voracious name and logo are trademarks of Hachette Book Group, Inc.

The publisher is not responsible for websites (or their content) that are not owned by the publisher.

The Hachette Speakers Bureau provides a wide range of authors for speaking events. To find out more, go to hachettespeakersbureau.com or email hachettespeakers@hbgusa.com.

Little, Brown and Company books may be purchased in bulk for business, educational, or promotional use. For information, please contact your local bookseller or the Hachette Book Group Special Markets Department at special.markets@hbgusa.com.

Book design by Mia Johnson

ISBN 9780316565059
LCCN 2024932894

10 9 8 7 6 5 4 3 2 1

IMAGO

Printed in China

CONTENTS

RELAX,

YOU'VE
GOT
THIS.

INTRODUCTION

The first time I fell in love with a piece of art, it was on the side of a train car

Growing up in Ladd, Illinois (population 1,300), my friends and I would sometimes wander down near the tracks to explore. There, in the middle of an overgrown field, we came across abandoned, graffiti-adorned train cars. They had an unexpected gritty beauty. I remember being entranced by the way the paint contrasted with the landscape — the bright colors against the rusty, muted metals.

That was ages ago, but I still feel that same thrill when I find an amazing piece of art. It's a sense of potential and wonder — the beginning of something. You see, while most people consider art a finishing touch, I look at things another way. After doing nearly a decade of design work, I've discovered the most natural way to create joyful, personal, livable, exciting, authentic spaces: start with the art, and build the room around it.

Art is the spark

Too often in interior design, art is an afterthought — the necklace you throw on as you run out the door. But I'm here to tell you, whether you're evolving an existing room or beginning with a blank slate: art is the place to start. It's the secret to a room with soul, and it's the ultimate road map to a home that feels deeply personal, warm, cozy, and special.

That's what this book is all about: breaking down the barriers so you can find and use art that moves you, and then build rooms that you — and the people you love — connect to deeply.

Affordable art is everywhere

So many people think that "good art" is out of reach — either it's too expensive, or it's simply impossible to find. But in reality art is totally accessible, and it can come from anywhere. It can be a flea market oil painting, a drawing your kid made, a sentimental piece of furniture, a collection of salt and pepper shakers, a five-foot fiberglass ostrich that charmed you at a vintage store (yep, she now stands tall in my living room — you'll meet her soon).

Art goes way beyond something displayed in a frame. Instead, think of it as anything that draws the eye and brings humanity to a space.

Creating rooms you love

As lead designer on the Magnolia Network show *Artfully Designed,* I've worked with dozens of people on home decor and learned that most folks feel intimidated by art. I want to change that.

My mission is to help you access the tools and the freedom to get comfortable choosing art, because it's the first crucial step in creating a home that truly reflects who you are. This book is my way of sharing everything I've learned along that path — including my secrets for hunting down treasures on any budget.

And my best trick? Building confidence so you can get out there and trust your own instincts — see magic in a tag-sale painting, recognize the potential of a gorgeous piece of fabric, spot a graphic poster or a stunning floor lamp or, heck, even an amazing shower curtain that can serve as the springboard to an incredible room.

We'll get specific

I'm a champion for artists and their work, in whatever form that work takes. I use my Instagram platform to highlight the incredible talent I've found in my community and beyond, and in this book I bring you many of my favorites.

You'll also get specs on designers I admire, paint colors I depend on, and shopping sources for all sorts of furniture and accessories — basically everything you need to make a room sing. This is not a rule book but rather a guide to help you navigate the design process, start to finish.

Ultimately, I want to help you discover what works for you, so you can do what makes you happy, do what makes you laugh, do what feels right. Make mistakes. Move things around. Become an expert on *yourself,* write your own rules, and confidently evolve your space.

When a space feels authentically *you,* you'll walk in and feel instantly at ease — right at home. And creating a space like that? Well, that's pure joy.

Ready? Let's go!

FOLLOW

PART
1

THE ART

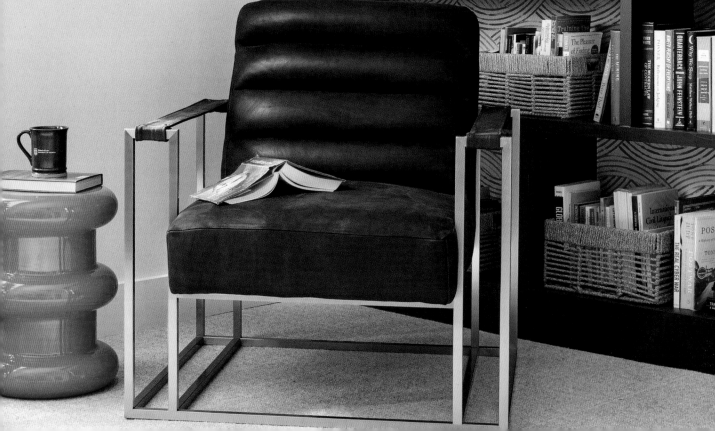

"BUT, NATALIE, I DON'T KNOW ANYTHING ABOUT ART..."

I hear this a lot. Sure, it can feel like art buying is a secret society that requires expertise or wealth (or both) for membership. But nothing could be further from the truth. So let's get those obstacles out of the way.

Obstacle #1: "I don't understand art..."

The big secret is that you don't need to. Choosing a piece of art comes down to one question: Does it move you? The advance work is tuning in to your own gut. I'll help with that.

Obstacle #2: " I can't afford art..."

Some art is expensive, but plenty of art is not. You just need to know where to look. I'll get into specifics later in this chapter.

Obstacle #3: "I don't know what my style is..."

You don't have to nail down your style before you buy art. Art is experiential. I can't always verbalize why a piece of art moves me. Sometimes it sparks an emotion — joy, melancholy, nostalgia, sorrow. Sometimes I'm drawn to the subject matter. Sometimes I love the color palette. And sometimes I have no idea why I like a piece. You don't have to be able to articulate your feelings. You can just love and appreciate art without being able to explain what's behind the feeling.

I'll help you get in touch with what you like, build your art confidence, and learn where to find art in any price range. Part of my mission in this book is to expose you to a huge variety of art so you can feel what speaks to you. But first, let's dig into who you are, and what you gravitate toward naturally.

WHAT ARE YOU DRAWN TO?

Forget trying to name your style. You contain multitudes! Instead, focus on the individual pieces you're naturally drawn to. Then you can start to think about how you can harmonize what you love. You can be a little bit country and a little bit rock and roll, ya know?

This chapter (and this whole book, actually) will help you identify what makes you tick — what motivates you and delights you — and how to use that insight in hunting for art.

Play up your quirks.

Fruit in art (and decorative objects) makes me smile. I have banana bookends, a strawberry stool, a pillow in the shape of cherries, and a plethora of pieces featuring oranges. I know that might sound weird, but it's what I love. What's your weird thing? Once you find it, amplify it in the art you choose.

Figure out what makes you *you.*

Understanding what you gravitate toward is the secret to finding art you love — and creating rooms that feel truly personal and joyful. Let's start with a little pop quiz. Now don't get sweaty palms on me! There'll be no grading. Think of this as a self-evaluation, a time to reflect on what you value the most. While these questions may feel unrelated to design, they can actually be quite helpful.

- What's your favorite food?
- What kind of music do you like to listen to at home?
- If you had a whole day free, what would you do?
- What's your favorite thing to wear?
- What are your three favorite items in your home right now? What do they have in common?
- What is your happiest memory of travel? (No limit on how many answers here.)
- Where (or in whose home) do you feel most at ease? Why?

Don't overthink it — just go with your gut and jot down your responses. You may be making use of this intel already without even realizing it. Does your favorite yellow dress remind you of the cabana stripes on that beach umbrella from your honeymoon? Let's take that further! When you're done, look for any common threads in your answers. When I took this quiz, it reminded me how much comfort and nostalgia play into all aspects of my life. What did you learn about yourself?

5

▼ I found this pretty pixie for less than $10 at a thrift store. And please note the oranges peeking in beside her.

5 WAYS TO BUILD YOUR ART CONFIDENCE

1. Keep an inspiration album on your phone. Getting your "art eye" going is simply about paying attention. Get in the habit of snapping photos of anything you're drawn to, from your lunchtime salad to the window display at a local shop to a cloud formation overhead. Keep an eye out when you're in nature, at a flea market, or in a restaurant, and grab a shot of everything you're attracted to. Add them to a Pinterest board or just keep them in an album in your camera roll. Nature, fashion, food — these are all part of opening your eyes to what you love. And of course, include actual art in this effort — if you see a painting or drawing or sculpture in someone's home, in your favorite café, at a museum, or on social media that makes your heart skip a beat, capture it. Swipe through your inspiration photos and look for common colors, themes, vibes. Are you drawn to landscapes? Graphic high-contrast visuals? Art with a sense of humor? Jot down what attracts you most. That's valuable insight.

2. Go on art outings. If you're intimidated by hunting for art, I challenge you to push your comfort zone and go on a field trip. Look to see if any local galleries or art schools are hosting an opening and plan an evening out with a friend. Or shake up date night with a walk through a local museum. These are low-pressure ways to explore new art without feeling the need to commit. See what draws you in, and take pics for your inspiration album.

3. Phone a friend. Imagine you're talking to your best friend about an outfit. You know how they somehow know exactly what isn't quite right or what would be perfect on you? Use friends in the same way for decor input. Ask someone you're close to how they would describe you in three words. This can be so illuminating. They can magically open your eyes to the way you see art and decor.

4. ABC: Always Be Collecting. You can gather art before you have the perfect spot for it — literally or virtually. I've got a Pinterest board for art I come across online and another called "Natalie's brain," dedicated to random inspiration. But I'll also buy art — or furniture — that really speaks to me before I'm even sure where it'll go. Five years ago I bought a credenza at Randolph Street Market in Chicago, and I only *just* figured out where to use it (as a vanity in my pool house). Of course you don't want to overwhelm yourself (or your storage space), so collect within reason.

5. Play around with easy-access art. Thrift stores and tag sales are the playgrounds of the art-minded. Illustrated books pulled apart, your kids' own art, great finds scooped up on trash night. Experiment with inexpensive art that's easy to come by, and you'll start to learn what speaks to you the most.

HOW TO FIND AFFORDABLE ART

Art is any piece that gets an emotional response from you. Look around. It's not just paintings; it's also gorgeous objects, textured wall hangings, flea market chandeliers. It's in the wagon wheel you find in an old barn and the framed needlepoints you unearth at a garage sale. There are spectacular prints and posters, amazing pieces for sale by art students, and those pillows your friend makes.

My favorite way to find art is when I'm not actively looking for it. You come across something unexpectedly, out and about or on Instagram; it snags your attention, and then it's impossible to look away. That love-at-first-sight moment. Shopping for art can become second nature. But if you're not used to it, it seems mysterious. It's not that different from shopping for clothes. Once you start thinking this way, you'll notice opportunities for art everywhere. Throughout this book there's lots of advice and info to give you a leg up on art shopping. Let me start you off with my personal cheat sheet.

INSTAGRAM: The best place to find art in all price ranges. Follow designers you like, then follow the artists they follow — and if you need help finding designers, start by following the folks I follow (see page 249). Then play the algorithm. Click on art you like, and the algorithm will serve up similar work.

FLEA MARKETS: Everything is negotiable. (But please be kind. These vendors took time to find these unique pieces, so keep that in mind when you're haggling.) If you can't get to the right price, walk away, and loop back before you leave. Also: look past the frames — sometimes it's easy to miss a diamond in the rough because of the wrong frame or a stained mat. Take your time.

ESTATE SALES: Same as flea markets. Play it cool and ask, "Would you take twenty dollars for this?" If the answer is no, come back in the last two hours of the final day of the sale. The key here is: *don't get attached.* If you can't help it and find yourself thinking about a piece all day long, maybe it's worth paying closer to the asking price.

LOCAL ART SHOWS: Galleries can seem intimidating, but the people who work there actually want to share their knowledge about the art and artist with you. Tell the gallerist or artist your budget — and be honest! This will help them help *you* narrow down your options. You can also ask if an artist out of your price range offers prints or sketches for purchase. Those are often cheaper, but the sale will still support the artist, and you'll still get to take home a taste of their work.

And don't forget about exhibits at local art schools and art-focused colleges. Amazing treasures to be had.

MUSEUM SHOPS: Prints and posters, when displayed appropriately, can be as elegant as a painting. Museum shops are also a great source for small sculptures, bookends (and books), tableware, and vases — reproductions for the win!

TRAVELING: Whether you're on a road trip or a business trip, talk to the locals (concierge at your hotel, barista at the coffee shop, friendly coed you bumped into on the corner) and ask if they can point you toward the local art scene — murals, art fairs, galleries. And once you find a treasure, *bring the cool thing home.* It's a pain, totally inconvenient, I know. But it's doable. And in exchange for one day of headaches, you'll get a lifetime of joy.

YOUR OWN HOME: Sometimes a piece just needs to move from one room to another. It's meant to become part of a grouping, or it's in need of a simpler frame. A fabulous chandelier might be more comfy in the bedroom than the dining room. A vibrant patterned rug that's buried under furniture in a bedroom might be drop-dead gorgeous in the living room. Playing with the art you already have is one of the most gratifying (and economical!) ways to launch an art-forward makeover.

Shop locally

There's nothing like seeing art in person. Whether you're on the hunt for something new or seeking inspiration from the local flavor, start by supporting artists in your community. To find artists or murals near you, search Instagram with your city name and the word "artist" or "mural" (say, "Milwaukee artist" or "Springfield mural"). This should pull up tons of options. Follow those that appeal to you, or save their page. Google to see if their work is displayed close by. If the artists are represented by a gallery, go check out that gallery's offerings. Visit in person if you can. You'll likely find pieces from other artists you are also drawn to.

START WITH A
PAINTING

The easiest way to decorate from the art outward is by planting a big (amazing) painting in a central spot. Once you ID a focal point that makes your heart sing, everything else unfolds organically. Look at this gorgeous piece by Kevin Sabo, in an equally gorgeous room by Theodora Miller. Instantly you can feel the sense of movement it brings to the space, how it adds warmth and joy (people dancing!), and how it boldly presents a room palette that might never have occurred to you otherwise (more on this on page 15).

This is one of my favorite lessons to share about decorating: when you find a painting that speaks to you, with the right mood, vibe, and energy, you've also found a map for the rest of your room — the keys to the kingdom. And here's another secret: The piece doesn't necessarily have to be big. It doesn't necessarily have to be colorful. It doesn't even have to be a painting; posters do the trick too. There are all sorts of ways this plan can manifest. In this chapter we'll explore tons of options.

PULL THE ROOM PALETTE FROM THE ART

Look at all the color connections between this painting and the room. Teal on the walls and ceiling give it the same backdrop as the art. Hot pink and orange in the rug and chair link with the limbs of the dancers. The green grass is picked up in the plants, and in a sculpture on the bookshelf. And neutrals — just as they do in the artwork — bring in some breathing space.

PAINTING + SETTEE: I discovered artist Erik Hoff at Randolph Street Market in Chicago. I picked up a piece of his for a client's house and asked if he had any new work coming out. He sent me a photo of three canvases in different color combos. I bought 'em all (see another, *opposite, bottom right*). I definitely took color cues from the painting, veering toward deeper jewel tones for certain elements.

PERFECT PAIRINGS

PAINTING + SOFA: This pairing speaks for itself. It's a one-two punch of style that frees you up to go neutral (or pile on more color!) in the rest of the room.

PAINTING + CEILING: You don't have to match your inspiration literally. For an unexpected connection, grab an accent color from the artwork and paint the ceiling a similar shade.

PAINTING + DUVET: If you're slowly transforming an existing room, make your art inspiration feel at home with soft goods while you figure out furniture. Bedding is perfect. Low investment, high impact, instant gratification.

A PICTURE'S WORTH A THOUSAND ACCESSORIES

Art has the power to create the mood for an entire room. This photograph by Emmanuelle Descraques (*left*), titled *Indiana and the Cigarette*, tells you immediately that this is a space to enjoy. I love a lounge — low comfy furniture, a cool, relaxed vibe, and a sense of personality. Notice how Indiana is framed by pattern — this draws the eye to her even more. She's the star of the show. *Right:* Every color in this graphic pop art triptych by Angela Chrusciaki Blehm shows up in the lively abstract rug, which unifies the space. This means the rest of the furnishings can be minimalist and sleek. Lounge perfection!

◀ The pale-blue outer walls pick up on Indiana's top. And the rug matches the drapes. No, seriously. It *does*.

◀ Another beautiful marriage of art and rug — and a great example of the power of art to set a warm and inviting tone. This living room, designed by Gina Sims, has a sense of excitement, but when you look closely at the furnishings, they're fairly simple. It's the art — and the palette connection (fireplace + trousers in the painting; chaise + top in the painting) — that defines the spirit of the space.

▶ A dramatic foyer sets the tone for what to expect in the rest of the home. This one is not tight-lipped about the fact that visitors are in for some fun. The art invites in a pair of red stools — more drama but also practical for an entry. Designer Diane Rath used temporary wallpaper here for a quick hit of style.

HOW A PAINTING TURNED INTO A ROOM

I call this living room in our home the Sprite Room, because the colors remind me of the cheery soda can. When I started designing this space, I never consciously considered this portrait — commissioned by my husband for me from the Chicago artist Natalie Osborne — but it was there in the back of my mind. When you find what you're drawn to, you'll notice yourself repeating those elements. As the room started to come together, it became clear that this artwork was my inspiration.

▲ Of course you can pull the main colors from a piece, but the influence can also show up in subtle ways. It could direct you to certain shapes, textures, and patterns. I mean, look at how the chandelier even mimics the earrings in the portrait!

ALL THE COLORS, ALL THE FEELS

You can use a painting to subtly suggest a palette, or you can *seriously saturate* a space with a close interpretation of a piece of art. For this inner sanctum, designer Michelle Fahmy took the second path. The dark walls echo the dominant color in the painting by Jacquelin Nagel and make the secondary colors — blue, gold, purple — really pop. These secondary colors make up the main palette for the rest of the room. Incorporating these shades in patterned elements (the floral bedspread, the graphic pillows) gives the space more dimension than it would have with blocks of solid color.

The room also references the subject in the painting, with a "body part" chair (a curved hand) tucked in an alcove.

HOW A PAINTING TURNED INTO A ROOM

When we moved into our home in Charlotte, I didn't have anything specific picked out for the guest bedroom. So I painted it a color I liked and then waited for inspiration to strike. Once I found this art, I knew I was ready to make moves.

I leaned into the interesting palette and textures of this piece. The camel-colored velvet chair is reminiscent of the subject's dress, the green of the chest of drawers mirrors that of the sofa, the cobalt-blue pillow comes from the painting's background shade, and the linear rug alludes to the lines on the sofa. Neutral walls — including diluted shades like this light blue — are the perfect backdrop to maximize the color punch of this beautiful painting.

▲ This piece by Mel Remmers provided more than color inspiration. The soft, drapey sensibility is something I tried to capture in this guest room, in furnishings, plants, and accompanying art.

PILE ON THE PATTERNS

To make a pattern mix work, think about the type, scale, and color of the patterns. Here you see an open, airy pattern with a white background on the wall, and a tight, densely colored pattern on the runner. These distinct elements harmonize because no one competes with another, and their shared palette unites them.

3 lessons from this space

1. **Let patterned art invite more pattern.** The framed textile was the inspiration for this space, and the "safe" choice might have been to forgo the graphic wallpaper. But the addition of the interwoven brushstroke design adds so much energy to the room. Plus, the patterned rug and stair runner bring in even more dimension.

2. **Use every color.** All four colors in the artwork show up elsewhere: dark green in the banister, red in the rug, and the blue . . . well, it's everywhere.

3. **Pick patterns that complement,** rather than compete. Here, the open, airy pattern on the walls harmonizes with the dense, intense pattern on the stair runner.

BRACE
FOR IMPACT

Bring a huge piece of art into any space, and everything changes. But in a room with challenging dimensions, like this one, massive art is even more impactful. Sure, it fills the large expanse of wall, but it also adds intimacy, bringing the eye down from the high ceilings into the lounge space.

And it clearly informs the palette, from the creamy white of the ceiling and rug to the spectrum of greens on the sofa, side table, and cabinet. Wood paneling highlights the neutrals and warms up the space.

Designer Katie Saro nabbed this treasure for just $25, but it wasn't easy. She couldn't quite fit it in her van, so she had to drive home with the back doors tied together with a strap. Bravo, Katie! I've said it before, but it's worth repeating — if you find something amazing, push yourself through the trouble of getting it home. You won't regret it!

SMALL ART IS LIKE A WHISPER...IT INVITES YOU IN

Bailey Schmidt, a painter with a background in printmaking and graphic design, constantly wows me. I used one of her small but mighty paintings as the starting point for this dining room (*right*). The graceful waves of the wallpaper, the soft curves of the oval table, and the "fingers" of the spindly chandelier all allude to the arcs and movement of the art. An almost neon element in the palette packs a punch — see more of the same in the piece above the fireplace (*opposite, top right*). The subject in this work by Malcolm Liepke will not be ignored. That chartreuse background? She is determined to draw you close. Never underestimate the power of a small piece!

◀ The orange Volkswagen bus among traditional elements is a reminder not to take things too seriously.

▶ While the terra-cotta wainscoting and turquoise sconce tie back to the retro graphic wallpaper, the Picasso replica stands out against it thanks to the grounding gray-scale background and punchier orange tone.

A PAINTING CAN FEEL LIKE A WINDOW

People are often scared of black paint, thinking it will make a space feel cold and dark. I think the key is to start with light, bright art. The effect is almost like installing a window. From there, matte black walls can feel cozy, not confining. This photograph by Robert Peterson, in a room in Iceland designed by Brian Patrick Flynn, brings both warm and cool tones into the space. It's hung low — just right to be viewed from the bed. The buffalo check throw and rustic lamp make this space comforting, not cold.

BEST SEAT IN THE HOUSE

◀ Cozied up to this epic abstract painting, a bistro table feels like the best seat in the house. For a chic cocktail-lounge moment like this at home, use a bright painting (hung low) as a dramatic backdrop.

▼ A classic landscape brings a breath of fresh air to a moody home office.

▶ There's a double take that happens with sky-blue art. At first glance it feels like a peek outside. The painted front door in this airy home has the same effect. And PS, catch the curves of the tulip table, pendant, and martini-glass marquee (in the art). Nice!

PAINTINGS IN THE PANTRY

(and other delightful design decisions)

◀ See Mick Jagger back there? He's permanently rocking out in my pantry, just off the kitchen, creating an exciting sightline from my breakfast nook. The way I think about it is, if I'm going to be in the pantry — or the laundry room or the garage — I might as well enjoy the vibe, right? Art makes every space (any space!) feel intentional.

▶ Utilitarian spots are low-pressure, so have fun, be brave, and move things around if your first try doesn't hit. Keep practical considerations in mind. In a full bath, for example, you don't want to hang anything too precious, because of the moisture — that's an ideal spot for a flea market find. But keep an open mind. You might just find the perfect painting for your laundry room and be inspired to go all out with a wall treatment that follows suit.

Does your art hang low?

▼ There's an awkward spot above my dog Billy's bed. It's only a foot or so off the floor, but because of the molding, it was begging for art. I upgraded it with his portrait. Leaning into the weird somehow made it less weird.

Incorporating your pets into the space makes it feel even more personal and lived-in. If you find something that reminds you of your current pet or one you had years ago, it's a special nod that only you might notice, but it makes the space more tailored to you. Even if you don't have pets, animal-inspired decor of all shapes and sizes can add warmth and personality.

Tips for placement and hanging

Where there's a hook, there's a way

Not every frame has to hang over a mantel. Experiment with unexpected spots — you might surprise yourself. Heck, I even hang art inside certain closets!

ALONG TRANSITIONS BETWEEN ROOMS: Cased openings (the frames of open doorways) are often ignored, but to me, they beam with potential. They can actually be the perfect spot to display little pieces of art that might otherwise get lost. Tiny art + tiny spot = perfect combo.

ON THE FACE OF A BOOKSHELF: This adds new dimension to the styling of a built-in and actually protects from clutter — you're less likely to keep stuffing things onto a shelf when it's highlighted by something you love.

LEAN YOUR ART: Nail holes can feel so final. If you don't know exactly where you want to put a piece of art just yet, prop it on the floor or atop a piece of furniture. Move it around the room (or from room to room) until you find the right spot — or continue doing it indefinitely to spice things up! Leaned art can also bring a casual vibe to a space; the same piece might feel buttoned up hung on the wall, but fun and playful when it's leaning.

START WITH A GROUPING

I met Jacques Pierre (as I lovingly call the Van Gogh–esque guy in the blue hat) at the Studio 8 Vintage shop in Forest Park, Illinois. I brought him home and hung him above the banquette in my kitchen. But he seemed lonely. Clearly, he was meant to be with a crowd.

I love a gallery wall like this one because it's very forgiving — if something feels "off," you can change one piece without dismantling the whole thing.

In this grouping, the mix of assorted framed and frameless canvases keeps it casual. Pops of color — like quince and gold — are fun to pick up on in the branches and flowers I add to the breakfast table throughout the year.

◀ It's nice to have company at the kitchen table.

The long view: Here you can see how Jacques Pierre and his posse work together to form a strong focal point for my kitchen. From a distance, a cohesive gallery wall functions like one large piece of art. This view also gives a peek into my living room, and another wall of art. Something to consider when you're hanging a grouping: What else shows up in the sightline, and is the mix compatible or overwhelming?

I love the way, from this angle, both the graphic rug and the geometric pendant point the way to the wall of art.

▶ With low groupings, accessories can become a fluid part of the arrangement.

Curate your groupings: I've already suggested you should Always Be Collecting (ABC), right? But that can bite you in the butt if you're tempted to jam everything you love onto one gargantuan gallery wall. Just as your gut led you to acquire the pieces that mean so much to you, your gut can help you know when enough is enough. Wise use of negative space is one of the things that makes a grouping look intentional and curated. It lets all the elements truly shine.

So KOC (Keep On Collecting), but don't hesitate to save pieces for later. The beauty of having some art in storage is that you can "shop" those whenever a room needs a refresh.

START WITH THE ART

5 TRICKS FOR GALLERY WALLS

1. **Identify an anchor piece** and build out from there. It might be the largest piece. It might be the most colorful (here it's both). It might be the most striking.

2. **Be intentional about palette.** White mats and frames on white walls = ultra airy.

3. **Think in clusters,** and vary shapes and orientation. See the tiny trio top left? Subgroupings make the whole greater than the sum of its parts.

4. **Mimic shapes in accessories.** Look how well the squiggly blue vase plays with the black squiggle on the wall.

5. **Take the colors off the wall** (of course). Sofa, throw, pillows, rug. Need I say more?

Negative space for the win

◀ In subject and placement, each piece feels very specific, like it's meant to be enjoyed one-on-one from a particular seat.

▶ A stairwell is a natural spot for an open, airy grouping of similar pieces in understated matching frames. With plenty of breathing room, the stars of the show are the colors and the faces.

3 TRICKS FOR TIGHT GROUPINGS

1. **Choose frames** of about the same thickness, but feel free to vary the width of mats.

2. **Keep the distance between frames** loosely the same throughout the grouping — and it's better to place them closer than you might think (just a finger or two's width between).

3. **Hang your favorite piece** at eye level, and take into account the use of the room — eye level in a dining room is lower than eye level in a hallway.

THE CRISP DRAMA OF A GRIDDED GROUP

▼ I don't think of myself as "traditional," but I do gravitate toward some traditional elements, like carved wood and marble. I find they can work well alongside quirkier things to bridge the gap between styles. Here I love artist Theodora Miller's grid of modern brushstroke paintings and chartreuse drapes mixed with formal elements — the oval-back chairs, a crystal chandelier, and the symmetry on the sideboard. A totally unique blend.

▶ I like to hang personal photos in a condensed area. I use the same frame and mat — sometimes in a variety of sizes — so that the assortment of eras and subjects feels cohesive and uncluttered. Keep it small or go big, like Jasmine Bible did in this epic stairwell (*opposite*). The uniformity of frames and monochrome color puts each print on a level playing field. Then as you get closer, you can hunt for memories of meaningful moments or familiar faces.

BUILD A GALLERY WALL AROUND YOUR TV

It's smart to incorporate a TV — the kind that lets you display digital art — into a gallery wall. It's a genius way to make the technology look intentional when it's not in use.

When you're starting with a big rectangle, it makes sense to think in clusters — flank the TV with groupings that can stand alone (because they'll need to when you're binging your favorite shows).

Breathing space on this gallery wall is what gives it a curated feel. See how there's some air between the central grouping and the elements on either side? All three zones would work well on their own — and together, against the rich dark-teal wall, they're spectacular.

THE SAME BUT DIFFERENT

Two of a kind

This duet is part of a series called Punch Buggies, by photographer Alexandra Tremaine, all shot in San Miguel de Allende, Mexico.

Three of a kind

You met this triptych in chapter 2. From this angle you can see just how hardworking art can be. It occupies one whole wall and is both exciting and unifying.

Four of a kind

When a room has great bones, you can emphasize that with the art. These mid-century panels by artist Bjørn Wiinblad represent the four seasons. They echo the lines of the picture frame molding in my Charlotte living room, imbuing the space with a comforting sense of order. I'm not a formal person, so I balanced their upright soldiers-at-attention presence with super-soft seating. The leather sofa, upholstered ottoman-as-coffee-table, and stools are cushy, low, and inviting.

START WITH THE ART

MESSAGE IN A GROUPING

Any grouping you assemble has meaning, but sometimes it's fun to pick a theme or send a message with a gallery wall.

My daughter, Maddie, is a strong, powerful girl, and in her room (*left*), I wanted to surround her with all sorts of strong, powerful girls and women. So we went with this grouping of portraits above the bed. (By the way, she also has an LED ice cream cone light because she likes ice cream — which is to say, I don't take my messaging too seriously.)

The gallery wall, *right*, by designer Brian Patrick Flynn, has a music thread throughout. It's also a great example of thinking cohesively about sightlines. The view through the wide doorway relates so well to the room itself. And look how simple the furnishings are. All the color comes from the art and the accessories.

◀ I have a thing for fruit in decor. Cherries here, strawberries in the bathroom (page 88). I just love it. As in art, in accessories I encourage you to play up your quirks, and go toward the things you love. It makes home even happier.

How to map out a gallery wall

● Get a roll of butcher paper (or grab a few paper grocery bags), a pencil, scissors, and painter's tape.

● Trace your frames onto the paper (also marking where the hanging hardware is located) and cut each one out.

● Use the painter's tape to position (and reposition) your stencils on the wall until the arrangement feels just right.

● Hammer or drill straight through the paper at the hardware mark. Then remove the paper and hang the art in its place. You'll save time measuring and leveling in the long run.

SURREALISM

VELOY VIGIL

START WITH
A MURAL
(WALLPAPER COUNTS)

I love murals because they can make any old space feel one-of-a-kind. A mural can bring energy and surprise and can also become almost a map for your decor. Look at this beauty designed by Gina Sims: the circle at top right is actually a wall sconce, with the bulb behind (note the glow) — it looks flat from here, so there's a bit of trompe l'oeil at play. The diagonal black lines on the mural pick up on the lines and angle of the banister. The stools, cabinet, and rug refer back to the palette and geometry of the mural.

You don't need a perfectly rectangular room for a mural, either. You can take your cues from the space, emphasize quirks, and work in (or around) anything in the way.

EVERYTHING EVERYWHERE ALL AT ONCE

Fully loaded. A dining room is the perfect place to go to extremes — layering pattern, paintings, 3D art, and spectacular lighting. In designer Gina Sims's Atlanta-area home, muralist Faye Bell hand-painted a custom mural in shades of blue and green. The cascade of brushstrokes feels almost like a waterfall — there's an amazing sense of movement. Dark teal above (ceiling) and below (baseboards) contains the energy beautifully. With gold-tone metallics everywhere — chandelier, mirror, sconces, chairs, frames — this room drips with glamour. But thanks to the funky portrait, offset in front of the mirror, it isn't at all stuffy. That hit of quirkiness really packs a punch. Oh, and best news ever: Faye Bell ended up turning this pattern into a wallpaper (fayebell.com), so now it's available to all, in a few different color schemes. There is something so satisfying about the color coming down the wall from the dramatic complementary ceiling.

GROOVY GRAPHICS: PERMISSION TO PLAY

The writing (and doodling) on the wall. My pool house (*right*) is meant to evoke the vibes of a vintage motel. I wanted it to be playful, summery, and celebratory, so I hired Buddy and Shelby of Canned Pineapple Co. to paint a mural that made my intentions very clear! *Far right:* This room originally had plain white walls. Designer Jasmine Bible chose to paint the ceiling black but felt that things were too stark. So she sketched a design, grabbed some paint, and added this squiggly art to the wall, instantly loosening up the vibe. The ocher sofa and thrifted painting above it soften the effect, while the striped rug answers back to the mural. So fun!

A MURAL CREATES MOVEMENT

Set a room free. I've been friends with muralist Racheal Jackson for at least five years. Her ability to infuse a space with joy via paint is extraordinary.

Racheal started her painting career when her children were young and she needed an outlet to let her colorful soul shine. Now she shares her talent on our Magnolia Network show, *Artfully Designed*. She lives in Oregon with her family but travels the country to install her graphic wall art in homes and businesses.

Racheal helped me take my den (*below, right*) from fine to finished in a matter of hours with an inspiring Candyland-esque ribbon of colors. It sits opposite a wall of bright-blue bookcases and serpentine wallpaper, so I wanted something to match the vibe in a simple way that filled the space appropriately.

Her very first mural (*right*) was both a labor of love and a couple's collaboration. She asked her husband, an artist himself, to draw a doodle, then re-created it on the wall to bring both their personalities to the space. I love the excitement of this playful wall within the neat, crisp lines of the kitchen. Warm wood on the ceiling and the floor acts as the perfect "frame" for this piece.

PLAY INTO WEIRD ANGLES

"I meant to do that." When you have a room with challenging architecture, lean into it. These stripes (also by Racheal Jackson) make awkward lines feel artful.

ENCHANT A SPACE

Create a sense of place. Take a look at this custom "listening nook" (*left*) that I created with some unused closet space. Frankie Zombie, also a member of the Three Musketeers on our Magnolia show, *Artfully Designed,* custom-painted this artwork to turn a nook into a supercool, purposeful mini room. Without this mural, this spot — full of potential — might otherwise just have turned into a pile of sneakers.

▶ In a bedroom, a mural at the head of the bed calls to the star of the show and says, "C'mon and dive in!"

▶ In a living room, a mural can make a soaring ceiling feel cozy and intimate.

DEFINE A ZONE

Who says you need to follow architectural lines? Create your own parameters with a print or pattern: a dreamy sleep nook (*opposite*), a mod backstop for a bar setup (*above, right*), or a playful rough-around-the-edges zone for casual entertaining (*above, left*). Make your own lines, and create your own parameters. Great lesson in all of life!

Above, left: Back in 2020, I was feeling homesick after having moved from Chicago to Charlotte. This sitting room off my bedroom had a wall with closet doors that made finding the right art challenging. So

I had a local artist (@swych19) paint right over those doors to create this tribute to both the place I had left and the place I had moved to: CHI for Chicago and CLT for my new home — the crown giving a nod to Charlotte's nickname of the Queen City. Graffiti is a hotly debated style. Love it or hate it, there's no denying it's all about personal expression. I love this representation of my story, which started in a small industrial town near the beautiful, gritty city of Chicago. Art should be something you feel in your bones, and I feel this mural deeply.

DIRECT FOCUS

Stylist Emily Henderson used this intricate nautical wallpaper mural (*left*) in her kids' play area. It feels magical and old-worldly, but also elegant — a plus, since it's on view from various spots on the main floor of the house. This scene came from Rebel Walls, where you can order murals scaled up or down so you can get the exact effect you want for your specific room.

Kristin Laing designed the two spaces shown here. On the left, she cleverly used ceiling-mounted curtains to draw the eye up and conceal the transition corner between mural and painted wall.

For the room above, she created a moody "library" with Ikea shelves, trimmed to look like built-ins and painted a deep teal, with a desk as the final puzzle piece.

SURROUND SOUND

Muted green woods gently envelop this bunk room. The designer opted to turn up the volume with lively green beds, rich blues, and strong splashes of fuschia, orange, and yellow. With space to sleep five and a playful mix of patterns, this is a room sleepover dreams are made of. And with wallpaper like this, a space is fully art-ed from the get-go.

DETAIL-RICH WALLPAPER FOR COZY SPOTS

Up close and personal. Intimate spots present the perfect opportunity for intricate wallpaper — art you can enjoy while getting ready for bed or putting on makeup. *Right:* Designer Rebecca Plumb was thinking "boutique hotel" when she created this guest room. Lush wallpaper with a dark background — picked up in the black bedside table — sconces instead of bedside lamps, and half a dozen colors from the wallpaper at play in the delicious mix of bedding make it feel like an exotic escape. *Left:* Diane Rath chose hot-air balloons for a kid's space. It's got whimsy, for sure, but is also sophisticated enough that it won't be outgrown in a couple of years.

WALLPAPER + CEILING: A LOVE STORY

It's all about the interplay. Get the feeling of going all out without going all out. Paper one wall and paint the ceiling a corresponding shade to achieve an enveloping feel. Use this trick to add drama to an entryway or bedroom or to visually connect adjacent spaces.

DECORATE FROM THE TOP DOWN

Oh what a feeling, pattern on the ceiling.
Wallpaper overhead has an amazing impact. And when you're lucky enough to have extra-wide crown molding (*left*), it works like a frame to really play up the pattern as art. For my daughter's bathroom ceiling, I opted for a beautiful floral wallpaper by Hygge & West.

I'm obsessed with cabana stripes — to me they feel like sunshine, vacation, joy. I went big here, with stripes of yellow and white tile. The green wallpaper was the perfect mate, softening what could otherwise feel cold and clinical. Stripes and florals are perennial crowd-pleasers.

At right, the wallpapered ceiling is the only pattern in the room. Its soothing movement makes the room feel almost as if it is underwater — a quiet haven (the workplace of a very organized mermaid, maybe?). It also reminds me of the swirls of certain cut stone — cool and textured, without being harsh. The main thing is, look how much more interesting this room is simply because of the ceiling. And notice how the color connections with the overhead wallpaper create a cohesive, satisfying effect that makes you say, "Aaaaahhhhh."

MY FAVORITE SOURCES FOR WALLPAPER

- Mitchell Black
- Cole & Son
- Graham & Brown
- Rebel Walls
- Hygge & West
- Schumacher
- Farrow & Ball
- Spoonflower
- Anthropologie
- Flavor Paper
- Chasing Paper
- Etsy
- Jungalow
- House of Hackney
- Rifle Paper Co.
- Serena & Lily
- All Modern
- Perigold

▶ *Right:* This vintage-style botanical paper is from my wallpaper line with Mitchell Black. *Far right:* This print gives off luxury boutique hotel vibes when paired with graphic tile, a modern vanity, and sleek brass accents.

▲ This beauty is named Beyoncé. As you can imagine, she's a major conversation starter.

START WITH AN OBJECT

My husband and I host what we call the Papier Pants Potluck Party. At this party, you wear whatever kind of crazy pants you want — the person with the best ensemble goes home with a trophy, naturally — and you can only bring a dish or drink that starts with the letter *P*.

Pineapple, Pringles, pale ale — we're not *picky*. The spread ends up being totally random and super fun. I look forward to this party, and it's always a blast. I'll never be a formal-dinner-party person. And I'll always be the person who, when she sees an amazing ostrich at a vintage store in Oak Park, Illinois, will haul it home and eventually build a space around it.

I encourage you to get swept up by the occasional unusual object — a sculpture, a vintage sign, an epic light fixture, a mammoth planter — and see what happens when you try it out in different spots around your house. While 3D art might seem a little more complicated than a painting or a poster, the principles are the same, as you'll see in this chapter. As you move through it, I hope you'll remember a fabulous find you have in your attic or basement or garage and be inspired to play.

ONE BRILLIANT PIECE MAKES THE ROOM

With a statement piece as a starting point — especially one that brings a smile — you're halfway to your design goals. This painted piano is one of my favorite things (our kitty, Boots, is another). I got so lucky on this one. A Charlotte photographer was shooting the work of local Black Lives Matter muralists to help them beef up their portfolios. She asked if she could bring this piece by Frankie Zombie into one of my spaces for the shoot. I immediately connected with Frankie (spoiler — we're now cohosts, with Racheal Jackson, on *Artfully Designed*). Later, after the team (and the piano) left, I couldn't stop thinking about it. I was terrified to ask how much it would cost but pushed myself. When Frankie told me his number, I was relieved it was actually something I could afford. I got a really cool, awesome, unique piece for a steal — and told Frankie to up his prices. Moral of the story: Ask what it costs. You may be surprised.

Legs for days. Intriguing, startling, and objectively beautiful, they add whimsy to a white space that is anything but boring. No problem mixing periods and palettes when there's something so off-kilter connecting them.

An unexpected squiggle.
Look how this wall-
mounted wooden sculpture
lifts the eye and animates
the space. You really never
know how magical a piece
can be till you try it. So if
you see something that
makes your heart jump,
grab it, whether it's a quirky
statue in a vintage store, a
modern sculpture, or an
amazing piece of driftwood
on the beach. Don't be shy.
Hang it up. Try it horizontally,
try it vertically. Move it to
another room. See what
happens. It might take a
little while for inspiration to
strike, so be patient, and play.

FLOATING ART: SPECTACULAR CHANDELIERS

Let there be lighting. Falling in love with an amazing fixture is a common condition of the design-obsessed. Three of the rooms to the left are in my own home, so you can see I suffer from the affliction. The white chandelier in my entryway (*opposite, top right*) comes from Stray Dog Design. The two tiers of floral papier-mâché are the right size for the soaring ceiling and stand out against the vibrant blue backdrop. The Gothic number (*opposite, top left*) in my living room gives a nod to the château style of the home and balances out the playful elements that surround it. And the sculptural modern fixture in my lounge (*right*) is from my own lighting line with Mitzi (I told you I'm obsessed). If you go gaga over a chandelier, grab it and hang it. Once you do, it's easy to experiment with art and accessories that match the vibe — see the dreamy sleep space (*opposite, bottom right*) — or charmingly challenge it: the yellow pendant in an art-filled entryway (*opposite, bottom left*) is sparring with other

"wow" objects in a lively bid for attention. Remember, a chandelier doesn't have to hang over a dining table. It can serve as the featured performer in just about any space — and all the better if there's a sightline that lets you admire it from afar.

FUNCTION + FORM =

Orange theory. It's lucky — and unusual — to have a chance to take your cues from a practical piece that begs to be the center of attention. I love the sculptural lines of a wood stove — modern or traditional. Here, the impact of this showstopping stove is multiplied simply by continuing its color across the ceiling. Fronds of banana leaves framing the deck door echo the majesty of the stove. Greenery warms up the minimalist space. The seating and rug — usually the center of attention — are in on the plan. You can almost hear them saying, "Okay, we get it — it's not about us."

SCALE UP

◀ **Six-foot marlin.** This fine finned specimen has been patiently awaiting its close-up. I finally found a home for him in my home office. The ceiling, painted Dynamic Blue (Sherwin-Williams), reminds me of a wave, so he seems right at home here.

▶ **Eight-foot palms.** I've got the opposite of a green thumb. When I walk into a greenhouse, I can feel the plants cower from me. They know. Any tree I've placed in this corner of my living room has died; finally I decided to cut my losses and get these canvas trees from House of Nomad in Charlotte. They remind me of Dr. Seuss's truffula trees. They're absolute showstoppers — everyone who sees them asks about them. And, even more important, they are perfectly safe in the home of any and all accidental vegetation slayers.

QUIRKY OBJECTS: MAKE 'EM POP...

▶ **Soft-sculpture hands.**
Textile artist Gwen Rucker makes these giant hand pillows, about two feet long (that's a normal-size guitar behind them!). They're at home on this bright orange couch but would also be spectacular in a minimalist, mostly white room.

◀ **Crayon heart.** Artist Herb Williams made this 3D piece out of hundreds of crayons. It hangs in my pool house — and yes, it smells just like a fresh box of Crayolas.

▼ **Pop art on matte black.**
This art piece featuring a paint tube in action makes a magnificent focal point.

◀ **Graffiti on white.**
A multicolored snowboard on a long, narrow transitional wall looks like it was born to hang.

...OR BLEND THEM IN

Can you spy the open-hand chair in the pic at right? Look how seamlessly it "holds" the room (pun intended). Floor, table, chair, frames, and distant cabinet are all of a piece. This is a whole other way to use an unusual object — in a way where you can almost miss it, but then when you see it, you're even more delighted.

Frame a sentimental something-or-other

◀ People often ask about family heirlooms that are not their style. They wonder what to do with them, how to incorporate them into their home. I say think outside the box — or *inside* the box, as in within a frame. This sweater-art that designer Brian Patrick Flynn hung in a dining nook in Iceland makes me smile. You can steal this idea to put a modern spin on your own special piece.

OBJECTS REPLACE ART

You can hang a painting over the bed . . .
oar you could lean into the beauty of a
functional object — especially if it lends
a soft theme — and allow that to inspire
your decor. In this Lake Tahoe
bedroom, the art-spot-of-honor goes to
a pair of painted oars. The room's simple
palette, recurring stripes (duvet cover,
upholstered bench), warm woods
(headboard, picture frames), and motif
of straight lines (art, lighting) all refer
back to the objects on the wall. I love
the subtle connection between the
chevron woodwork and the chevron
paddle stripes. So satisfying.

TAKE AN UNUSUAL OBJECT TO THE NEXT LEVEL

It can be so hard to start from utter scratch. With my most recent reno project, contractors were headed my way with hammers swinging, and I was still looking at inspiration photos and unwilling to commit to a plan. That's when I realized that I needed to take a step back and accept my own advice. I'd identified my inspiration. I'd collected things I loved that still didn't have a home. Why not start there?

So I went to my garage and found a piece of furniture I always thought would make a great vanity and asked my contractor if he could retrofit it for me (*far right*). That piece turned into one of the foundational elements for the space and a jumping-off point for the rest of the design. Once I realized that I could build off something I already owned and loved, the plan started falling into place.

I got six of these line-drawn panels (*above*) — used by a textile company in the 1960s or '70s for trade-show displays — for just $200 on Facebook

Marketplace, without a plan for where I'd use them. I had been mulling over adding wallpaper to my guest room, but worried about it competing with the wallpaper that already lived in the hallway. That's when it occurred to me: the panels! Leaned behind the bed, they have the drama of a mural with the flexibility of a painting — I can move them anytime I want. But I doubt I will, because they turned out to be the perfect backdrop for the space.

START WITH A COLLECTION

When people ask what I find myself collecting, I have a hard time answering; for me, the better question would be "What *don't* you find yourself collecting?" I'm drawn to so many things . . . wooden fruit, seashells, fortunes from fortune cookies — I've been collecting them since I was a kid and now probably have enough to decoupage an entire coffee table.

Even if you're not a hunter-gatherer, you may have some collections by default. A set of glassware passed down, a million Pez dispensers that have taken up residence in your home, a shelf full of beloved LPs.

Is your grandmother's china sitting in a box gathering dust? Rather than reserving it for special occasions, display it year-round. Or (and I'm speaking from experience here) reframe your view of your son's baseball hat collection by arranging it along a wall in an artful grouping.

Is there something you can't pass up when you see it in the wild? What's your thing? Cultivate it — and use it to create a room that's totally you.

START WITH THE ART

Collected items can be sprinkled throughout your home to add quirk, sure, but showing a collection all together gives you a chance to make a big visual statement. One of the best (and easiest!) ways to let a colorful collection shine is to use white as a canvas. This rainbow of glassware (*left*) also benefits from built-in shelving — a natural frame. There's something so satisfying about seeing a collection contained this way.

Warm wood, subtle metallics, and a hit of nature are all that's needed to complete this space. Dramatic and welcoming, all at once.

▶ I love things with faces on them and inadvertently have amassed a substantial assortment: antique pincushion heads, sculptures, plates. Each has its own unique personality — truly. When I use one while styling a shelf — among the more functional items like books and baskets — it's almost like adding a person to the room.

START WITH A COLLECTION   115

A COLLECTION
OF BASKETS

Sure, baskets can sit stacked somewhere and come
out on an as-needed basis. But make them the
feature of a room, and you might just come up with
the glue that ties everything together. A wall of
swirly pattern and texture defines this space, where
wovens and wickers abound — the pendants
overhead, the coffee table, the throw pillow. It's a
small space with a lot going on, but it's all connected
thanks to the textures, colors (that bright blue), and
pattern (cabana stripes from the ceiling down to the
seating) woven throughout. No matter what you've
collected, identify the characteristics that you can
incorporate in other elements throughout the space
to tie it all together.

Decades of box office ticket stubs, matchbooks
from favorite restaurants, even jewelry — items
en masse, no matter the size, can be impactful.
Small, meaningful collections can sit on a shelf
and activate your memory bank when you
see them, while providing texture among your
other decor.

A COLLECTION OF ALBUMS

My taste in music varies widely — I don't think I can choose one artist or type as my favorite. But I think that's the way it is with a lot of things, including design. You don't have to settle on just one genre of music, just like you don't have to settle on one style for your home.

While much of your artwork may have a loose link to who you are, collections can send an overt message. Over the years, I've used records, band posters, even framed ticket stubs, to turn people's passions into art. You can do the same for yourself.

◀ A book ledge is the perfect perch for a record collection. Keep it static, in a cohesive palette, or change it up. This homeowner does a seasonal swap of album covers on display (here, they're all red for Valentine's Day) or displays according to theme. Every time the albums change, the feeling of the entire space changes.

▶ Since formal dinner parties are not in their repertoire, these homeowners opted for a casual combo dining space / listening lounge, utilizing their huge LP collection as "actionable" art.

KID CLUTTER OR ARTFUL COLLECTION?

It's all in the spin. My son, Kellen, loves hats, shoes, music, baseball, and video games. He has every single one of those elements incorporated into his room in different ways. His favorite hats are on display, he's got a Pac-Man LED light, a pillow on his bed that features two of his favorite bands (the Doors and Queen), a Cubs blanket, and his favorite baseball memorabilia on shelves. A common color palette prevents the room from feeling too chaotic. And being deliberate about potentially messy collections — like his hats, displayed in a loose circle that has room to expand — brings a sense of order to the space.

Passions don't need to be translated literally. You can use them as a starting point.

◀ Sports fan? Consider ways to incorporate something both functional *and* meaningful into the space to represent that passion. You could keep it literal by tacking a Red Sox jersey on the wall, for example, or give a nod to your love of baseball with Fenway-green lockers or vintage stadium seats instead.

TREAT EVERYDAY OBJECTS LIKE A COLLECTION

I love a home that feels personal. Give me all the books, family photos, and giant jars of shells you've collected along your travels — that's how I can tell you *live* in your house. Every grouping of objects, no matter how small, is an opportunity to be artful.

Play favorites. There's no rule that says books have to live on a shelf. Style a surface with books organized by color ▶ that can play well with a graphic piece of art. Or pluck titles that have special meaning to you ▲ and stack them in a place of honor. It's nourishing to make eye contact with books that speak to you throughout the day, even if it's just a glance as you pass by.

◀ **A bright frame.** Designer Cathy LeVitre literally highlighted her delft china collection by painting the display cabinet yellow and adding a striped pattern as a backdrop. The contrast between the traditional china and the primary stripes is so striking.

3 CLEVER WAYS TO DISPLAY SAME-WITH-SAME

A fun and easy way to build art confidence is to collect a specific type of affordable piece that you're drawn to and that's easy to find. Small landscapes, pet portraits, botanical artwork. It helps develop your eye while it gives you some "inventory" to work with. Similar pieces naturally hang together (pun intended) on display, so it's a win-win.

1. Theme a small room. Equestrian prints are the show ponies of this powder room (*right*). Precision gives like items a powerful presence. For advice on hanging a tight grid like this, see page 53.

2. Wrap a corner. Designer Gina Sims playfully arranged a collection of paint-by-number landscapes (*opposite, top*) by layering smaller pieces above larger "anchor" paintings. That's what gives the display so much texture. When hanging an evolving collection, leave yourself plenty of room to grow.

3. Puzzle together a wall. Be loud and proud with your display — particularly if the items are substantial in size or quantity. Plaster a wall with framed postcards or posters. If you've got a ton of inventory at the start, plan out your arrangement on paper first. Or hang three of your biggest pieces, then build out your grouping from there. Don't fret over imperfect edges in the grouping — it gives a carefree, yet curated, effect.

START WITH A TEXTILE

When I spotted this multipanel wall hanging at a vintage place in Chicago (Dial M for Modern), I could not take my eyes off it. The full piece is huge — probably around fourteen feet wide. I didn't use every panel here, just what fit the space (my entry) best. That's a great lesson, actually: if you love something that seems way too big for your life, consider whether there's a way to modify it. Just like you might tweak a dress, you can alter textiles (and, in fact, furniture — flip back to my retrofit of a credenza into a vanity on page 111) to suit your space.

Rugs are literally art for your floor! But there are so many other manifestations that get ignored: wall hangings, window coverings, bedding. They're tactile, soft, warm, inviting — and just waiting to make a one-of-a-kind splash.

TAKE LIBERTIES WITH WALL HANGINGS

A wall hanging is any textile you choose to hang on the wall, plain and simple, whether it's a formal loomed piece of art or slouchy printed burlap sacks.

▶ *Clockwise from left:* Vintage coffee sacks in a home in Iceland designed by Brian Patrick Flynn; a colorful abstract weaving interacts with fronds of potted plants; a large stormy "landscape" made moodier by the rough-hewn wood that anchors it; my former living room, where a southwestern rug on the wall helped ground the orange-yellow-tan palette.

WINDOW TREATMENT AS ART

If a spectacular oversize window is the clear focal point of a room — as it is in this home office — start there, with a patterned curtain or roman shade; it's essentially a huge piece of art. Here the view is extra emphasized with a white frame. Paint colors — plus the golden wood — connect directly to the window treatment. When raised, it shows off the view. When lowered, it adds texture and excitement and energy to a space of mostly solids.

◄ Whether used as a floor covering or mounted and matted, rugs are art. A handwoven piece with organic edges makes a particular impact in this room with modern clean curves and a two-tone paint treatment.

▶ When layered atop a larger rug, the tufted tiger in my living room stands out and adds an extra quirk factor to the space.

HOW A
SCARF
TURNED INTO
A ROOM

▲ I love the movement of this abstract floral design. You can almost feel it spin.

A while back, I saw a decorating article with an amazing piece of art over the fireplace. Turns out it was a framed vintage scarf. I added that to my running inspiration board and went on with my life. A couple of years later, I was in a mid-century furniture warehouse with a client when I saw this framed vintage scarf. I made it mine and saved it for just the right project (spoiler alert: it turned out to be my own dining room).

I wanted this dining area to be a space where people would feel enveloped in a rosy glow — a spot to linger and talk for hours.

We use our dining room constantly for family games, homework, and grown-up work — I knew we didn't need some kind of off-limits space that only got used on special occasions.

To evoke a warm, welcoming vibe, I pulled the salmony rose color from the scarf for the ceiling. To counter the boxy elements — the molding, door, table — I took inspiration from the curvy lines of the scarf and chose organic, curvy chairs. I think the combination — and the low, cozy bistro chandelier — is ultra inviting.

3 lessons from this space

1. To make a room cozy, "lower" the ceiling with a rich color.

2. You don't need a lot of art — just the right art.

3. A storied rug can break from the room palette and still feel right at home.

BRING IN A SOFT BACKDROP

Add instant character on a large scale in a renter-friendly and often budget-friendly way with fabric. The backdrop gives the same effect as wallpaper or a mural.

◀ Emily Henderson draped this offset stripe with a polka-dot reverse to act as a joint "headboard" for a pair of twin beds.

▶ Amara Hasham repeatedly wows with two wallet-friendly murals made from everyday objects: a throw blanket (*opposite, top left*) and duvet cover (*opposite, bottom left*). You could use a shower curtain to achieve the same effect.

DESIGN

PART
2

PRINCIPLES

WHAT DECORATORS KNOW ABOUT COLOR

Waking up in a cold sweat thinking about paint is not unusual for me — this is evidence of just how much importance color has in my life. For me it evokes a mood, a feeling, a memory, an energy — a sense of peace or excitement or joy or calm — not to mention offering a feast for the eyes. The excitement of combining colors to transform a space makes me giddy. This is my happy place. I want to share it with you — empower you to experiment with colors you love, mix it up, make a room or a wall or a piece of furniture completely yours. In this chapter, we'll identify colors that instantly speak to your heart, discuss why certain colors naturally work well together, reevaluate shades you may have written off — and bring all that info to a practical, actionable place, with specific paint recommendations.

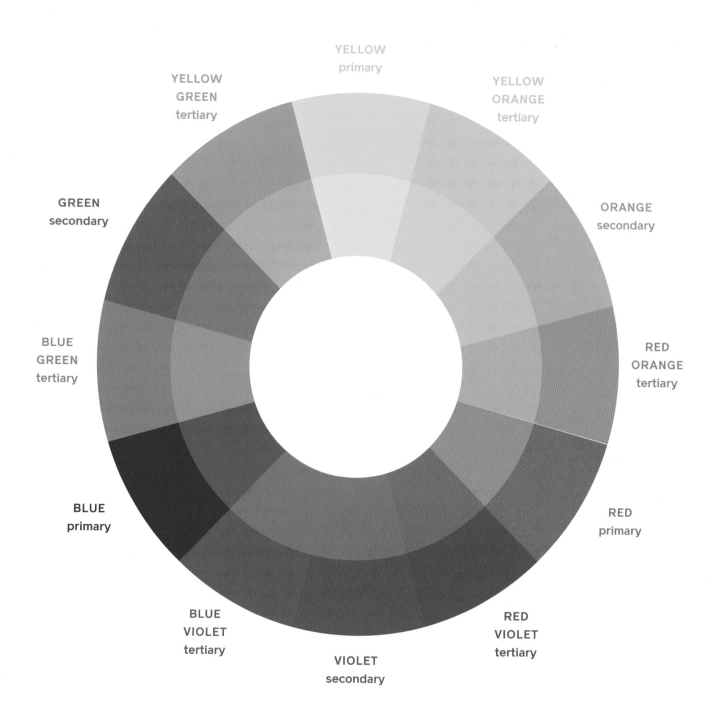

YELLOW
primary

YELLOW
ORANGE
tertiary

YELLOW
GREEN
tertiary

ORANGE
secondary

GREEN
secondary

RED
ORANGE
tertiary

BLUE
GREEN
tertiary

RED
primary

BLUE
primary

RED
VIOLET
tertiary

BLUE
VIOLET
tertiary

VIOLET
secondary

HOW TO USE THE COLOR WHEEL

Remember your first box of crayons? You opened up that fresh twenty-four-pack and went wild. There were probably a few shades you reached for immediately — colors you were naturally drawn to. Then you met the sixty-four-pack, which was both mind-blowing and enlightening. You learned more about yourself. While you didn't particularly like Vivid Violet, you were crazy about Wisteria. Burnt Sienna was okay but Melon really lit you up.

Time for the grown-up version of that awakening: the color wheel. Sir Isaac Newton created the color wheel in the seventeenth century, mapping the color spectrum to illustrate the relationship between shades. Do you *need* to know all about the color wheel to create a beautiful space? No. But it can be super helpful if you're into it. I'll break it down, and you can utilize whatever helps. Here are the basics.

- The wheel's foundation is the three **primary** colors: red, yellow, and blue.
- These primary colors can be mixed to create three **secondary** colors: orange (red + yellow), violet (red + blue), and green (blue + yellow).
- Mix one primary color (say, red) with one secondary shade (say, orange) and you'll get a **tertiary** color that fills the gap between the two (in this example, a brick-like reddish orange).
- The color situated opposite a certain hue is that shade's **complementary** color (yellow is the complement of violet, for example). You can always count on them to work well together.
- Color **neighbors**, those that sit *next* to each other on the wheel, are also complementary (like yellows and greens, or blues and violets).

OPPOSITES ATTRACT:
orange-red + light blue

Take away the orange-red accents in any of these spaces, and you've got a beautiful blue room — some shades soft and subtle, some punchy and powerful. Add back in the fiery shade (with a rug, a bed frame, a chair), and it instantly grabs the eye as a focal point. Magic, right? The unexpected dollop of color from the opposite side of the color wheel makes each room feel livelier and more fun.

145

NEIGHBORS COLLABORATE:
green + blue + violet

Look at the color wheel and you'll see violet next to blue, which sits next to green. Look at this beautiful room and you'll see the same, in action: malachite-green paint, sapphire blue in the wallpaper, amethyst bedspread. This "neighbors" principle works with saturated tones, like you see here, as well as muted versions of the same. That's one of the fun things about working with color; you can play with the intensity to get different effects.

BUST OUT
OF YOUR
COLOR
COMFORT ZONE

With hundreds (thousands!) of paint shades to choose from, how do you ever narrow things down?

Start with your gut. Go back to the crayon box, and think of those favorites you reached for again and again. Peek in your closet. What are the colors you gravitate toward in your wardrobe? That's one way to start identifying your preferred palette.

If you want to stretch your range, play "paint chip poker": Go to the paint or hardware store with no goal in mind. Stand at the wall of paint chips and pull a handful of colors you like without thinking — at least ten. Take those swatches to a table and start putting them together. Then narrow your uninhibited palette down to five or so shades.

Exciting, right? It's fun to loosen up and open your eyes to new color combinations. Snap a pic and save this palette in your inspiration folder.

Another route: Look through the rainbow of options on the following pages, and pay attention to your gut responses. How do the colors make you feel? Do the saturated shades make you do a double take and reconsider your reliance on neutral paint schemes? Notice what you're drawn to, and what surprises you. This is the way to get outside your wheelhouse (in a good way) when it comes to color.

CHERRY TOMATO, BY SHERWIN-WILLIAMS

The orange-red on these cabinets raises the temperature of the room — especially impactful in a small space. Black and white are the perfect foils.

REDS & BOLD PINKS

Stop signs are red because they're meant to catch your attention, right? Red can be very dramatic and literally halt you in your tracks. Choose the right red for your space, and it will make people pause and take a closer look.

RED PEPPER, BY BEHR

A saturated brick red can combine with blue and white without skewing too Fourth of July.

GYPSY PINK, BY BENJAMIN MOORE

An energetic pink can be edgy and vibrant. Used in a home office, it offers pure rev-you-up-to-work energy.

CORAL BEAD, BY SHERWIN-WILLIAMS

This warm bubble-gum pink screams "Barbie's grown up. She's got bills to pay and a business to run." It's timeless and feminine, but not overly sweet.

ORANGES & YELLOWS

Citrusy shades instantly liven things up and make it hard to feel anything but happy. Even if you wouldn't choose one to roll across all four walls, you might find it's just right in a supporting role, giving your space some serious character.

AZTEC BRICK, BY BENJAMIN MOORE

This shade says, "Look at me," and makes you want to pay attention to what's displayed on those shelves.

TRINKET, BY SHERWIN-WILLIAMS

A rich gold on the ceiling creates a pseudo skylight that instantly lifts the spirit.

BUGLE CALL, BY VALSPAR

My favorite color is marigold. It can be energizing or help you decompress. It is my personal happy place.

AUTUMNAL, BY SHERWIN-WILLIAMS

Warm but soothing, this color suits a bedroom beautifully. It's like a sunset in a paint can.

153

LAZY CATERPILLAR, BY BEHR

This dense, rich shade can turn a transitional space into a showplace. Look how well it highlights art — especially in colorful frames.

GREENS

The range of options can have immensely different effects. Whether you're looking to create earthy natural vibes or make a striking statement, consider greens — they might surprise you.

NOTTINGHAM GREEN, BY BENJAMIN MOORE

A cool green can be as upbeat and pleasing as mint-chip ice cream. Use it to balance out warmer elements.

CURRENT MOOD, BY CLARE

This green gives off a mossy, organic energy. Used on the ceiling as well as the walls, it envelops you with a sense of ease.

MATCHA LATTE, BY CLARE

Green is the color of clover, a symbol of good luck. How can you feel anything but lucky and alive walking into a space that surrounds you with this shade?

BLUES
& PURPLES

Sky, ocean, wildflowers — this color
category can conjure natural elements
or offer high drama. It's all about the
level of color saturation. Exude the
mood you want and beat the blues with
these options.

NEW YORK STATE OF MIND, BY BENJAMIN MOORE

It's hard not to love this classic
academia blue. It's always a win, and
can be especially striking juxtaposed
with white.

SKY FALL AND JARGON JADE, BY SHERWIN-WILLIAMS

As swatches, these similarly
saturated hues give off an
Easter-egg vibe. But with the
black-and-white curtains and
wood beams here, the effect is
super-sophisticated.

GRAPE ICE, BY BENJAMIN MOORE

Not every shade has to be full-saturation. This barely-there lavender tint makes furnishings pop while balancing the warm tones of the wood floor.

BLUE BOUQUET, BY VALSPAR

Light blue is relaxing. Keep it from skewing too sweet by combining it with dark, moody accents (like the striped ceiling and tufted leather bench).

CLEAR MOON, BY BEHR

A true modern white can sometimes appear almost blue and feel cold. Whites with a hint of yellow (like this one) have more warmth.

WHITE(ISH)

My go-to uniform is a white shirt and jeans, because I can add pops of color and instantly make a fun, unique outfit. White is one of my favorite paint colors for the same reason. It provides a restful canvas for artwork and furniture and lets your personality shine through.

DIMPSE, BY FARROW & BALL

This shade reminds me of a crisp white museum wall: fresh, clean, and makes everything look special.

TURBINADO, BY CLARE

Beige has never been my favorite (there's a reason for the #banthebeige hashtag). But the right beige in a curated space is a surprising breath of fresh air.

MALTED, BY BEHR

The hint of pink in this blush beige feels like a warm hug. It's feminine and classic at the same time.

WATCH IT WITH THE SWATCHES

I was recently deciding on a palette for my guest room while sitting outside in the sunshine. I thought I'd found a group of colors — yay! Then I took the swatches into the actual space (which only gets afternoon light) and instantly realized they were not going to work at all. These colors were vibrant and lively outdoors, but in the guest room they felt dreary — they would have made the space feel dark and cavernous.

It's so important to look at swatches in context and observe them at different times of day to see how the changing light (or lack of light) affects them. The reality is, tiny swatches don't tell you much, no matter what. To truly understand how a color will behave in a room, you've got to go big. It's not difficult. Some options:

1. **Oversize swatches.** Many paint stores offer eight-by-eleven-inch (or so) swatches of individual colors. Check with yours.

2. **Big decals.** Online companies like Samplize offer large swatchlike decals that you can stick, peel, and move from wall to wall. Genius.

3. **DIY painted poster board.** To see your picks on an even larger scale, get some poster board from the dollar store and paint it with a pint-size sample, then tack it up.

3 PAINT "CANS"

1. You CAN dilute or enhance a color.

When you find a shade you like, but it feels a tad too saturated or not saturated enough, typically you'd move to the next color on the paint deck. Sometimes, though, those adjacent shades are nowhere near the same tone. If you've ever said, "I just want a color between these two," you can make your own! Take the swatch to the paint store and ask them to make a sample that's lightened or darkened by a percentage until you get it just right.

2. You CAN paint just the woodwork.

Painting trim, doors, or banisters can offer a big payoff without a major buy-in. Opt for something at least a few shades darker than your current wall color. (I love a melon pink on the trim with barely-there blush on the walls.)

3. You CAN recover from a paint fail.

A while back, I decided to paint my white entryway (*above, left*) a vibrant blue — walls and ceiling. I loved the color in small doses, but — oy!— on every surface, the effect was overwhelming. I decided not to be too hasty and immediately paint it back to white. I lived with the blue for a bit so I could really identify what worked and what didn't. Ultimately, I decided to repaint about a third of the walls the original white (*above, right*). This way the foyer

serves as a colorful focal point but also connects to the white walls of the adjacent rooms.

When narrowing your choices, give yourself time to live with color samples for a bit, whether you paint the color on poster board, hang decals, or slap the color up on one whole wall. Also take comfort in knowing that if you do goof up, you can change it. Sure, repainting is not free, but it's not a huge cost either.

DESIGN PRINCIPLES
FOR EVERY ROOM

My first — and favorite — design principle is
to start with the art. From there you can take
things in so many directions. This chapter
walks you through eight more maxims that
make it easy to unlock the magic in virtually
every space.

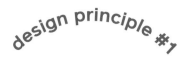

design principle #1

DREAM BIG

Forget about finances for a minute: What's your reach-for-the-stars vision for your space? Seriously, no holds barred. Let loose. This is a fun exercise (and reality will always be there when you're ready to get down to business). Look at your inspiration file and unlock your creativity. Are you craving rich graphic wallpaper? A spectacular light fixture? Something playful like a swing or a hammock? Jot it down. While you may not be able to achieve your entire vision from the get-go, you'll tackle what you can and build the rest over time. These days, you can find quality options at practically any price point — you just have to be willing to hunt. Take your time, and you'll get there! Make sure you know where that is, but allow for big visions from the start.

PLAY UP A ROOM'S BEST FEATURE

Before you make any big changes to a room, take a minute to ID and appreciate its natural resources. Make the most of what's already there, whether it's a beautiful tin ceiling, interesting tile, or a wealth of sunshine. If you find, for example, that you gravitate to a particular spot in the morning because of the light, that can be extremely illuminating (pun intended); let it help inform how to set up — and use — the space. Identifying the positives will help you determine where to focus your efforts. *Left:* Enhance a sun-drenched corner with bright white paint and an eye-catching window treatment. *Near right:* If your space has a built-in palette thanks to interesting tile work, use it as a color map for the room. *Far right:* Simplicity is sometimes the solution when you've got beautiful architectural detail.

DON'T BE AFRAID OF THE DARK

The quickest route to a moody, captivating room is a deep, dark color on walls *and* ceiling. Dramatic? You bet. Scary? Doesn't have to be. Just know going in that this move will radically transform the space, so don't get attached to other ideas until you've painted. That cozy, cocooning effect makes a big statement — and does much of the heavy lifting, decorwise. Depending on the use of the room and the overall vibe you're going for — formal or loungy, say — you may find you need less furniture than you thought. Color can sometimes take up space. Don't fight it. Just let the color help you figure out the rest of the room.

▶ **On the other hand, white is not a cop-out.** Want the opposite feel? Think of a yoga studio, and the light airy neutrals you'd see there (versus the intense tones of a spin studio). White paint is a perfectly legit choice, especially when you have lots of light or a dramatic piece to showcase, like the canopy bed here.

AVOID THEMES, CREATE VIBES

▲ **How the West was won.** I did this office for a client in Charlotte. Her favorite place is Sedona, so we painted an abstract landscape in a warm terra-cotta—that was enough to conjure the vibe of the West.

My daughter, Maddie, loves the beach. When we were designing her room (*right*), we went with soft shore-inspired colors and a brass-and-seashell chandelier. After those two literal hits of beachiness, we pulled from other inspiration, with wicker chairs and a garden mural. Rather than using a theme, we focused on creating a feel.

Other ways to do ocean without going overboard (ahem): use that funky seashell mirror you found at a thrift store, incorporate sea-green throw pillows, or bring in a sea-breezy candle. Maybe you just need a single painting of a sandy landscape to help transport you. No need for a "Life's better at the beach" sign (however true that may be).

The point is, keep it subtle. If a theme washes over every single element, it can turn kitschy. When you layer in items from various areas of inspiration, your complexity and character come through — and the result feels ultra personal.

SOMETIMES MORE IS MORE

I love pattern and color, layers of personality and joy. Our den (*left*) is bright and playful, with plenty to look at — meaningful objects, practical pieces (TV, big clock, pillows for extra seating on the floor), and big blocks of color. The secret sauce? Black and white, as a grounding element. On the rug and on the wall, the patterns connect without competing, so the room feels exciting but not stressful. While homing in on your inspiration is key to creating a room that speaks to you, it's just as critical that you consider the space's purpose. Form and function should be part of the same thought. This is where we watch TV, so a comfy couch and cozy rug are must-haves.

Do you have a dining room that's rarely touched? Think about what you could do to make the place appealing for other activities. I'm not saying you need to chuck the dining table, but how can you add elements that make you go into the space more?

▲ **Whole lotta living goin' on.** Decorated to the max, this space has a happy lived-in feel that invites casual conversation, plopping down with homework, and pulling out board games. What helps it look artful, not chaotic? The calming palette.

SOMETIMES *LESS* IS MORE

▲ **Perchance to dream.** The mostly monochromatic palette of this soothing space makes its hits of blue ultra impactful. Designer Rosie Case managed to create warmth with a cool color scheme and minimal accessories.

Coco Chanel said to look in the mirror on your way out the door and take one thing off. That's not necessarily my style, but in decorating it can be the answer to certain puzzles. Occasionally you'll find that something just isn't working in a space, or after years of hanging on to a piece, you have yet to find a use for it. In these cases, that may mean it's time to let it go.

There is a practical side to getting rid of things, sure (more space for new stuff you love!), but it can also be emotional. Ultimately, you have to come to terms with the fact that the item served its purpose for you and will be better utilized by someone else than collecting dust in your basement.

So if you're working on a space, feeling like something isn't quite right, or just itching for a change, subtract. Take some pieces off the shelves. And if you're just starting to work on a room and it seems to be begging for less, add one element at a time. Negative space will help highlight the items that do earn a spot of honor in the room's design.

▼ This kitchen's decor comes down to a mere three choice elements: statement pendants, punchy stools, and a graphic runner. The end.

GARNISH WITH GREENERY

You've painted, you've hung artwork, you've laid out the furniture. Now what? That's easy: Add life! I never consider a room complete without plants. Real or faux, plants offer shape, movement, and fresh color. Heck, even fruity shapes (see that lemon planter, *right*?) bring a sense of vitality to a space. But don't stop there. There are many other ways to bring life to a room. Sprinkle in family photographs, make use of animal motifs, and pop in objects with faces or features (see my vintage mannequin friends on page 115, and the "eye" pillow on page 225).

IF YOU LIKE IT, IT'S GOOD

Designer Kate Pearce says this space (*left*) — with optical-illusion printed wallpaper overhead, deep-burgundy walls, and tomato-red seating — is her favorite in her home . . . and her worst-performing on Instagram. Evidence that what works for one person doesn't work for everybody. I have two words for you:

Who. Cares.

Your home should make *you* happy — and of course those you love and share it with; they get a vote too. But it's definitely not about what anyone else thinks.

So, even if a "rule book" tells you to use black and white as a grounding element in rugs, if you have a vision, do the opposite and put it on the ceiling (*right*). If it looks good to you and makes you happy and fills your heart when you see it, it's the right choice. "Good" is entirely subjective.

NATALIE'S
NOTEBOOK

Over the years, I've identified a handful of
elements that have a huge impact on the
overall feel of a home. This chapter breaks
them down. It's meant to guide you in making
your entire home feel unified and inviting,
while ensuring that each individual spot is
special and personal.

TIE NEARBY ROOMS TOGETHER

So you've finished your living room design, only to plop down on the sofa and realize that the adjacent dining room (which you can spy from your plush perch) doesn't quite jibe with the space. How do you connect rooms? The instant fix: identify a piece of art or decor that you can put in the dining room to tie the two together — one that pulls colors from both rooms, say. In the future, rather than thinking about one room at a time, consider the adjoining areas and how they can play nicely together. The sightline from my dining room into my kitchen has the advantage of a continuous warm wood floor. But I also like the way the art and decor connect. The muted palette of the kitchen gallery wall connects to the wallpaper running up the staircase, which ties into the terra-cotta ceiling in the dining room.

START WITH THE ART

▲ A rich rust-toned wall highlights the view into a glamorous bathroom with a related blush texture.

▲ Greens in the art and honey-colored wooden frames connect a white hallway with a green-all-over home office.

▲ Similarly, blue-patterned
wallpaper invites the eye into the
deeper saturated tones of this dining
room, where Queen Elizabeth gets
the Warhol treatment.

STYLE
STORAGE
INTO YOUR
DECOR

Elaborate wallpaper makes shower
essentials (in the cabinet) look orderly by
comparison. When you have visible
storage, think about what surrounds and
abuts it. A happy pattern sets you free — it
means you don't have to stress about
making practical items look perfect. As
long as your paint or wallpaper plays well
with the colors of your "mess," it feels
intentional and unified. That's easy in the
bathroom: just choose towels, bins, and
jars that pull from the palette of the walls,
tile, or cabinets.

◀ **Nothing to hide.** Sure, books are great on built-ins, but so is barware. Feature your prettiest glassware, artful bottles that adhere to your palette, and a special piece of art.

▲ **Same idea.** Show the pretty stuff — colorful books and globes — and stash the less aesthetic items. Matching bins in a neutral print not only hide a multitude of sins but also easily link to subdued sophisticated accessories. A storage wall painted partway up creates some parameters, adds to the sense of order, and connects beautifully with the bedroom wall.

CREATE AN UNFORGETTABLE ENTRYWAY

You know what they say: You never get a second chance to make a first impression. Your entryway is an opportunity to express who you are with a "wow" moment. This is a great place to be a bit *extra* with your style: wallpaper, patterned tile, a spectacular light fixture, and just a couple of truly special pieces of furniture and art. Think of it as the most curated spot in your home (sans the shoes).

Consider the experience of walking up to a home: based on the exterior, you may not know what's in store. But with a thoughtfully designed entryway, the moment you step through the door? Boom. You get it.

◀ The entrance to my home (which I've lovingly dubbed the "Charlotte Château") is pretty grand, with its curved doorframe, high ceiling, and picture-frame molding. I opted for a two-tier chandelier to fill the tall space and arranged a vignette front and center. Leaned art allows me to play and swap new pieces in and out as the mood strikes.

▶ One of my favorite things is an entry packed with meaningful art. This dense gallery, alive with color, picked up in the storied runner, conveys a lot about the spirit of the people who live here. I love the intimacy of this. The dramatic pendant gives an amazing view from a distance and plays up the beautiful lines of the iron door.

LAYER LIGHTING SOURCES

It's all about variety. If a room has too much of one thing — say a surfeit of floor lamps, or nothing but table lamps — it runs the risk of looking like a lighting store. Been there. The solution is simple — and, actually, also practical. Make a conscious choice to vary light sources. Some floor, some table, maybe some sconces, and an overhead. Also think about the way the light shines — you want uplights and downlights, tiny lamps for tiny spots, and the option of ample wattage wherever reading might occur.

Layered lighting is a major component of a comfortable room. It gives you so much flexibility: Spotlight a mini moment with a table lamp. Flip the switch on a floor lamp to warm up an intimate conversation zone. Dim down a stunning chandelier to create a sense of intimacy in a dining room.

Up, down, side to side. Layered lighting makes every space more inviting and more functional. It also presents opportunities for style hits. Can you imagine the rec room on page 198 without the cubist lantern pendants? Neither can I! Cover them up and see what a difference a lamp makes. In my "sunrise room" (*far left*), the overhead fixture reminds me of a parasol, which is something I find myself drawn to in life and in art. Parasols are so utterly charming. I also love to dot a home with sculptural table lamps, like the vintage-inspired number (*right*) from my line of lighting with Mitzi.

DISPLAY PERSONALITY, FRONT AND CENTER

We used to go to Florida when I was a kid. We'd play in the sand, buy delicious food from the hot dog stand, and have the best time with our grandmother. I remember sitting on the beach with my grandma on the last day of my first visit, feeling like I never wanted to leave. We just sat there talking, and it became one of those unforgettable perfect moments.

I never got over my love of that place, and I never stopped wanting to re-create that feeling in my own home. Recently I had the chance to. I converted our garage into a pool house, inspired by pool houses of vintage motels. That meant cutting a bar window into the back wall, painting the concrete floors with a checkerboard design (page 68), and putting up

green-and-white tile (inspired by cabana stripes). Voilà: Our very own Florida beach hot dog stand, ready to provide comfort food and a sense of ease to everyone who visits.

My favorite spots in anyone's home are those where you see exactly who that person is — whether that comes through in personal photos, books they've read, or an interpretation of a place they love. Access that.

Close your eyes and think of a favorite place. What do you hear? How does it smell? What do you see? Is it specific colors? Is it a certain type of light? Mine that information, and show it in your home. It will make you happy every day.

Show off your quirkiness. Designer Elsie Larson says folks are incredulous when she explains that she amassed this collection of books over time — choosing titles based not only on color but on content — and that she didn't simply cover books in scrapbook paper to create this "wow" moment. But it's true. Each book made it into Elsie's home because it appealed to someone in the family — *and* it made a color statement. It took years. Elsie calls the endeavor a lesson in patience. I'll say! On floor-to-vaulted-ceiling shelves, it's also a lesson in super-unique design.

Show off your skillz. I've bragged about my *Artfully Designed* cohost Racheal Jackson a number of times — she's a rock star, and one of the most inventive and talented people I know. She's truly a Jane of all trades, and when she gets an idea, she goes for it. Here's a shot of her kitchen. Rather than painting the island, Racheal created a Lego wall that ties in with the nearby mural and celebrates her family's playful sensibility. If you've got it, flaunt it!

MAKE BIG STATEMENTS IN SMALL SPACES

When you really want to pack a decorating punch, bigger may not necessarily be better. There's so much potential in small, practical rooms — they're easy to conquer and complete, and they have the power to bring joy every day. Consider the small spaces you have where a bold design could have a major impact. Bathrooms, laundry rooms, even closets can benefit from wow-worthy wallpaper, statement fixtures, or bold swaths of color.

An added benefit? Budget! Because there's less space to decorate, fill, or paint, you'll get the drama you crave without a huge investment.

Dense decor. This kitschy desert-resort wallpaper (*left*) gives a nod to simpler times and is a great match for other mid-mod elements, like the terrazzo countertop and wainscoting on the lower half of the wall. Power-packed design in a tiny space. More examples: A powder bath (*right*) exudes old-world charm with an idyllic mural and a magnificent repurposed vanity. Modern stripes, moody blues, and poppy posters create an energetic space (*below*) that makes laundry feel like less of a chore.

PROBLEM-SOLVERS

If you find yourself stalled out, I've got you.
What's your hiccup? Here are answers to the
decorating questions I'm asked most often.

"What makes sense in terms of where to splurge and where to save with decorating?"

It's personal. A lot has to do with where you are in life. Ten years ago, with a puppy and two young kids, I went budget all the way. (I didn't need to spend money on a nice table or couch when I knew my kids were going to spill grape juice on it.) Now, though, I would splurge on a rug I love — because I'd keep that a long time — and save on things like pillows, because I tend to swap them out so often. Make your own rules, and remember you can change them anytime.

"How do I decide what to keep?"

Flag the sentimental stuff. You won't want to get rid of pieces with real meaning to you (but be judicious — don't hang on to a lumpy worn-out couch just because it brings back memories of Christmases past). Then shop your home like you would peruse a store — moving items from one room to another can have a big impact. Then you can see what you need to add. Sometimes simply replacing bedding and floor coverings can give a space an entirely different feel. Also, remember what a difference a new layout can make. See if a new furniture arrangement solves some of the challenges. That can completely change the way you see the space — and it might just highlight exactly what needs replacing and what deserves to stay.

"How exactly do you take the colors of a painting and interpret them in a room?"

It's not an exact science. But there's a lot to learn from the proportions artists use. Carrie Gillen is a Saint Louis–based artist whose work I find incredibly inspiring; she uses color combos I'm not normally drawn to, but I love them in her work. Take the piece in the middle right of this grid. Now

that could be a moment in interior design! One way it could play out: eggplant ceiling and trim, black-and-white wallpaper, soft blush rug, and unexpected greens and blues in throw pillows. A great way to begin: Look at an existing piece of art in your living room, and help it make sense by adding an accent pillow, planter, or lamp in a similar shade. Then build slowly from there.

"What if my taste differs from my family/spouse/roommate's?"

Mix and match. Sometimes the hunt for the right pieces is like trying to answer the question "What do you want for dinner?" Everyone is likely to have their own idea, and it can feel like a challenge to marry "flavors" in a way that pleases all involved. In your home, you might find the solution within a single piece — say, a sofa with a mid-century silhouette (to satisfy his taste) in a bold graphic print (to satisfy hers). Other times, it may come from the unique way a collection of varied elements are incorporated within the home. Personality-packed vignettes like this one can be a great solution. With each person's style represented, everyone can feel a sense of connection to the space.

"My room just doesn't feel... done. What should I do?"

Paint a door. Sometimes the fear of going overboard can make a space feel unfinished. If you're lucky enough to have nice architectural detail, the easy answer is to add a pop of color by painting a door (*below, left*), the ceiling, or some molding.

In my bedroom (*below, right*), I painted my ceiling black, and it actually gives the illusion of height, making the space feel more expansive. Mantels, stair risers, and banisters are also favorite spots of mine for black paint — it's practical as well as pretty, helping to hide dirt, smudges, and shoe marks.

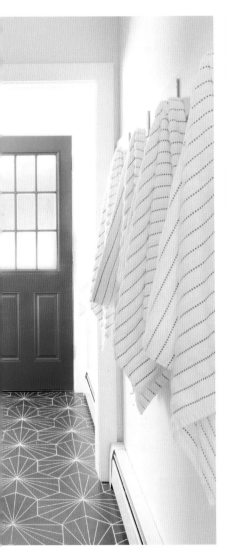

"But, Natalie, I'm in a rental."

Don't let that stop you! If renting came with a list of commandments, #1 should be "Thou shalt not hesitate to decorate." If you can't paint, don't fight the beige — just let it be your story's canvas. Lean into art and accents: rugs, pillows, blankets, decorative pieces, books, lighting, collections — even temporary wallpaper.

"What if I want to sell my house someday?"

Live for today! Unless you're actively thinking of putting a For Sale sign on the front lawn, please (PLEASE!) just surround yourself with the things that bring you joy. Don't overthink it. Five to ten years from now, you may sell the house. But right now, it's your haven, so design a space you truly love.

"I don't have the budget to buy new stuff. What do I do?"

Start with pre-owned. Consider vintage or thrifted furniture before particleboard placeholders. With a little hunting, you'll get better quality at good price points. Alternatively, swap the hardware on your existing furniture for an easy (and potentially even cheaper) refresh. Try out new drawer pulls on a well-loved dresser or revamp a desk with fresh knobs. And when it comes to art, reframe the situation (literally). Swap out the frame on an existing piece to make it feel more luxe or change the way it interacts with the space. You'll create a new look without as hefty a price tag as an entirely new piece.

"It's taking so long to find the pieces I need. How can I speed this up?"

Be patient. My biggest tip for you as you bring a space to life is not to rush it. Step back and analyze the room as it's coming together, just like you might assess a meal as you're cooking it. Rather than simply tossing in all the ingredients at once, sample it along the way to see if it needs anything. Add seasoning to taste.

"I have heirloom pieces that just don't feel like me, but I feel guilty getting rid of them."

Revamp to reuse. A friend of mine has a collection of doilies her grandmother made. She couldn't bring herself to get rid of them but had no clue how to display them — or if she could even convince herself to do so. We put a few of the doilies in floating frames, painted her kitchen teal, and hung the frames in an asymmetric pattern. She loved it. We were able to take something antiquated and make it modern, honoring the history but putting my friend's stamp on it.

"I have this decorated room, but no art, and I want to zhuzh it up."

Introduce a surprise. While I love the idea of starting with the art, we all know that things may happen the other way around. But look at it this way: a room in need of art represents a huge opportunity for drama.

Get a load of this stunning equine making a casual entrance into a calm, neutral living room. It makes you stop and say, "Whoa, Nelly!" And it completely transforms the space.

The secret to success with an art surprise like this: pick a piece that works within the parameters you've already created — but is extra on one level. The palette of the horse photograph is right in keeping with the palette of the room. But the *scale* is a total surprise.

"I can't put my finger on it, but something in my space feels 'off.'"

Take a picture. Occasionally, you'll find that you've collected all this fun stuff you love, put it into your space, and . . . it's just not working. But you're not sure why. Fashion stylists will take a Polaroid of an outfit to assess the facts rather than the feelings. And it works with rooms too. Snap a pic — this allows you to look at the individual components *and* the combo in a fresh way. You'll see things differently, and you'll be able to spot what needs tweaking.

"I'm not confident about styling. How do I do it artfully?"

Create mini moments. Think about where in your life you are most adventurous: Do you love to travel? Are you fearless with fashion? Channel that confidence, and recruit those skills. If fashion is your forte, you might add excitement to a beige blazer by pairing it with a wildly patterned scarf. Do the same at home by bringing a dash of bold pattern to a space dominated by solids. If you're more the explorer type, give a basic bookshelf some personality by incorporating items that remind you of your favorite locales.

Decorating doesn't have to be a one-and-done sport. If you find that you enjoy styling and restyling, your rooms can always be in play. Bring home new treasures or resurface old ones, create vignettes, zhuzh up corners — and evolve whenever you please (just for fun or seasonally). By giving a small section a refresh every once in a while, you'll give the entire space a whole new feel.

"My room is boring. What's the quickest affordable fix to spice things up?"

A graphic rug. Spread out a statement floor covering and you've got something with major visual impact that doesn't necessarily cost a fortune. In a dining room, opt for a flat-weave rug below your table (*left*) so chairs can slide easily and inevitable crumbs can quickly be hoovered up. In a bedroom, you may choose something a bit more plush to add coziness.

"I fell in love with some wallpaper, but it's too expensive for my (large) bedroom. Help!"

Just do one wall! You don't have to take wallpaper corner-to-corner or floor-to-ceiling — make your own rules! In my bedroom I used this awesome wallpaper mural (*right*) as a "headboard" in the alcove where I tucked in the bed. If you can't afford the paper you want right now, get a small sample and display it in a frame until you can save up for a full wall.

"What kind of art is safe in a bathroom? I'm worried about the moisture."

You don't want to put anything precious in a full bath. It's the perfect spot for something fun from a tag sale like vintage magazine pages or framed wallpaper scraps. I'm not generally a DIYer, but for one of our hallways in our Chicago Victorian, I found a vintage coloring book of Victorian homes and had each family member decorate a page. I framed those and hung them down the wall. The purpose of art is that it has meaning to you and your family. Is there some creative spin you could take to make unique art for your bathroom?

"What's the secret to a good mix of throw pillows?"

My standard recipe: Mix solids with prints of varying scales (skinny stripe and bold floral, perhaps) and unify them with a common palette. Toss in an outlier, like a surprising color or quirky shape to round it out. You can get really artful (*above*) or keep it super simple. If you're nervous about it, one matched pair pulls it together, no matter what.

"I'm planning a kitchen reno and want to make it special. How can I add some style?"

Look all around for inspiration. I was at a coffee shop in London, and my eye was drawn immediately to the subtle glimmer of a brass strip under the countertop. It was such a unique way to create interest between marble and the cabinetry beneath it. This is my kitchen in Charlotte. I asked my contractor if we could do a brass band beneath the marble. He said he'd never done it before, but he didn't tell me no. So I ran with it! He set an extra surface on top of the cabinets before placing the stone so he could have something to attach the brass to. It continues to be one of my favorite elements in the space.

Moral of the story: When you see something unique that gives you that "Ooh! Ahh!" feeling, take a picture, and consider how you might be able to interpret it in your own space.

WHAT MAKES THIS ROOM WORK?

Sometimes you see a room that *just feels right*. Use that gut reaction as your cue to dive deeper into the *why*. I love Pinterest and Instagram as much as anyone, but image overload can make us freeze, or have us copying exactly what we "like" instead of following our own design path.

Rather than looking at a photo in your feed and saying simply, "I love this room," take a moment and see if you can ID the elements within the space that you're drawn to. Is it the sofa? If so, what about it? Is it the fabric? The shape? The scale? Don't just take an image at face value — analyze what it is you like and how you could potentially get the same feeling from your own space. When you notice the visceral response and dig into the components that sparked it, you're halfway to creating rooms you love.

Splash of fun

The combination of modern and traditional elements in Orla Read's Notting Hill bathroom jumped out at me. A traditional claw-foot tub updated with a blush-pink exterior feels surprising — and there's so much excitement in its proximity to the striped shower tile.

Round and round

I'm drawn to the art, light fixture, and interesting circular treatment on the ceiling. Designer Kimille Taylor obviously took cues from the curves in the artwork and architecture when selecting elements for the space. But I love how she included an angular coffee table in opposition to those curves to give the eye a place to land. This space provides a good reminder that the architecture of your home may drive design decisions. Lean into it!

Natural neutral nursery

I was instantly drawn to this room by Lacy Hoysradt when it came across my feed. Why? I'm not designing a nursery. These aren't my typical colors. But the shape of this light fixture alongside the earthy toned fabric struck me as so peaceful and serene. It got me thinking: How can I take these two elements that pull me in and use them in a space of my own to create a similar mood?

JEWEL BOX WITH A VIEW

Black ceiling for coziness

Elegant wallpaper framing out the room's focal point (the bed)

Showstopping fixture that encapsulates the room's palette

Surprise punch of color

Curves on furniture and textiles to soften the drama

Warm wood everywhere

AHEAD
OF THE
CURVE

Something cool to look at overhead

Dark drapes for drama, privacy, and sleeping late

A painting that explains the palette

Built-ins to hide essentials and promote calm

Warm + cool colors playing together on hard and soft elements

Sconces keeping bedside surfaces clutter-free

SUGAR AND SPICE

A tiny galaxy on the ceiling

Long curtains mounted high to make windows feel taller

Dark giant sofa softened by plush blush and cream textures

Lush velvet to balance tough leather

Earthy palette pulled from painting and amplified

GROVE COVE

Lacquered ceiling = more light

Scalloped pendant creating a strong sense of place

Orange trees bringing sunshine, life, abundance

Inviting café components

Comfort in cabana stripes

Honey-colored wood

HOTEL
AT HOME

Grounding-but-exciting
black-and-white pattern

A feminine touch beside
"menswear"-inspired bedding

Sumptuous velvet headboard
as standout statement piece—
made extra special as the sole
hit of green in the room

Strict symmetry to anchor a
mix of lively patterns

Warmth in the form of wood—
and favorite books

Color neighbors that tie in with
the rug, lamps, and wall

A worn, inviting feel to balance
all that precision

LUSH MINIMALISM

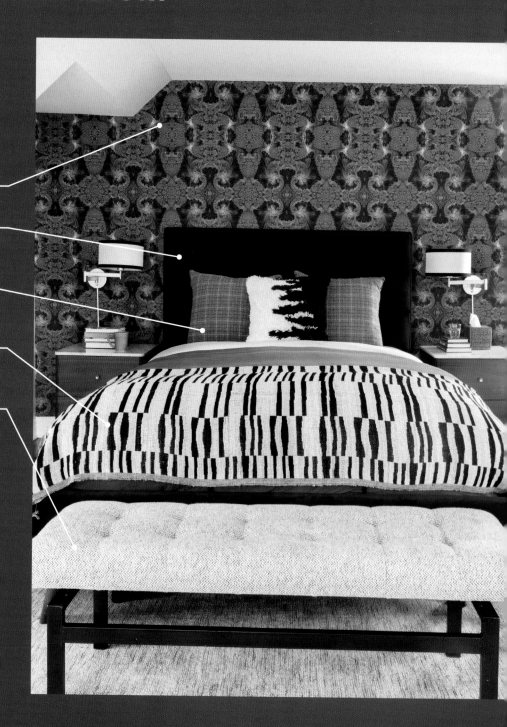

Rorschach-esque curves

Luxurious velvet

Satisfying symmetry

Quirky pattern breaking
up solids

Artful choices for practical
pieces

SIMPLICITY WITH SOUL

White to highlight strengths: large windows, slatted walls, fireplace

Softening shades in art and accessories

Hits of mid-century magic

Low, easy vibe

Weighty stripes grounding an airy look

ARTISTS, GALLERIES, AND DESIGNERS

If you're not sure where to start hunting for art, here's a list of folks who may inspire you, spark your imagination, and get the gears turning. Go down the rabbit hole! You'll find something you love and can afford. These are some of my current favorite artists, Instagram accounts, and sources of inspiration — but it's just the start. I'm always looking, continuing to discover, finding inspiration in new avenues. Hopefully this list will kick-start your own discovery.

Remember: This journey will continue throughout your life, so keep your eyes open. Your house doesn't ever need to be "done." It's an evolution. Use your space to make yourself and your loved ones happy and comfortable in the stage of life you're currently in. Evolve as life changes. There are no real rules, except this one: Decorate for today . . . and change it up tomorrow.

Inspiring Instagram accounts

Alexandra Swistak / @alexandraswistakart

Juniper Briggs / @juniperbriggs

Frankie Zombie / @frankie.zombie_

Garrison Gist (Paint Can Papi) / @2gzandcountin

Bekah Worley / @bekahworleyco

Golsa Golchini Art / @golsa.golchini

Sally Podmore / @sallypodmoreart

Picchiarello / @picchiarellopixelart

Patrick Puckett / @patrickpuckett

Rachael Van Dyke / @vandyker

Brooke Lancaster / @brookelancasterart

Justin Ellis / @jus10_ellis

Bailey Schmidt / @baileyschmidtart

Holly Keogh / @hckeogh

Angela Chrusciaki Blehm / @angelachrusciakiblehm

Racheal Jackson / @banyanbridges

Buddy Norton and Shelby Lowe of Canned Pineapple Co. / @cannedpineappleco

Margo McDaid / @margoinmargate

Liz Kamarul / @liz_kamarul

Juliana Lupacchino / @ju._lu

Daniel Freaker / @freakerstudio

Michael Hedges / @michaelhedgesart

Joe Kameen / @joekameen

Ria Krishnan / @riakrishnanfineart

Emily Van Hoff / @emilyvanhoff

Wolffia Inc. (Emily Jackson) / @wolffiainc

Grace Stott / @gracestottt

Natalie Osborne / @natalieodecor

Guzzo Pinc / @guzzopinc

Peter Keil / @peterkeilart

Frances Berry Moreno / @where_is_frances

Brenna Peterson / @brennalp

Brittany Smith / @brittanysmithstudio

Stacy Kiehl / @stacyk_paints

Connor Liljestrom / @connor.liljestrom

Ashley Mary / @ashleymaryart

Jen Matthews / @jenmatthews_art

Denise Hughes / @denisehughes_art

Michel Van Devender / @michelvandevender

Ron Giusti / @mrgiusti

Nico Amortegui / @nico_malo1

Mione Plant / @mioneplant

Marianne Angeli Rodriguez / @marianneangelirodriguez

Marina Savashynskaya Dunbar / @marina.sd.studio

LaurieAnne Gonzalez / @laurieanneart

Jessica Moritz / @jeszmo_art

Angie Barker / @angietherose

Windy O'Connor / @windyoconnorofficial

Emily Keating Snyder / @emksnyder

Stephanie Lear Henderson / @stephaniehendersonpainter

Jan Skácelík / @restyleart

Maria Macarena Luzi / @macarenaluzi

Erik Hoff / @commonorder

Bertille de Lestrade / @darlingtoutim

Jo Tilker / @jotilker_art

William LaChance / @wmlachance

Anna Blatman Studio / @annablatman

Dee Clements of Studio Herron / @studio_herron

Molly Odom Magill / @cliffandcallahan

Farron Feiner / @farronfeiner

Kevin Chupik / @kevinchupik

Katie Lebel / @katielebelmakes

Parsons People / @parsonspeopleart

Victoria Villasana / @villanaart

Erin Hanson / @erinhansonartist

Trish Andersen / @trishandersenart

Herb Williams / @herbwilliamsart

Kent Youngstrom / @kentyoungstrom

Kenny Nguyen / @kennynguyenclt

Erica Avila / @ericaavilaart

Jill Ricci / @jillricciart

Stephanie of An Abstract Woman / @an_abstract_woman

Claudia Marchetti / @claudiamarchetti_art

Miguel Ángel Fúnez / @miguel_angel_funez

The amazing designers, photographers, and artists whose work appears in this book

Cover: Designed by Natalie Papier of Home Ec. (@home_ec_op), photographed by Megan Easterday of Easterday Creative (@easterdaycreative)

p. i: Designed by Natalie Papier of Home Ec. and Kelsey Diane Design (@kelseydianedesign), photographed by Megan Easterday of Easterday Creative, art by Alexandra Swistak (@alexandraswistakart), wallpaper by Mind the Gap (@mindtgap)

p. ii: Designed and photographed by Natalie Papier of Home Ec., art by Valerie Feo (@soval_art)

p. v: Designed and photographed by Natalie Papier of Home Ec., art by Frankie Zombie (@frankie.zombie_)

p. vi: © Flynnside Out (@bpatrickflynn), photographed by Robert Peterson (@rusticwhiteinteriors), art is vintage

p. viii: Designed by Natalie Papier of Home Ec., photographed by Megan Easterday of Easterday Creative, art by Peter Keil (@peterkeilart)

p. xi: Designed and photographed by Natalie Papier of Home Ec., art is vintage

p. 1: Designed and photographed by Natalie Papier of Home Ec., mural by Racheal Jackson (@banyanbridges), wallpaper from Etsy (@etsy)

p. 2: Designed by Gina Sims Designs (@ginasimsdesigns), photographed by Cati Teague Photography (@catiteaguephoto), art by Edward Ruscha

p. 4: Designed and photographed by Natalie Papier of Home Ec., art by Lisa van Wijk (@weebza)

p. 5 (top): Designed and photographed by Natalie Papier of Home Ec., art by Carolyn Joe Daniel (@carolynjoeart)

p. 5 (bottom): Designed and photographed by Angela Chrusciaki Blehm (@angelachrusciakiblehm), art by Angela Chrusciaki Blehm, Juliet Blehm, and Hayley Mitchell (@hayley_km)

p. 6: Designed by Natalie Papier of Home Ec., photographed by Megan Easterday of Easterday Creative, art is vintage, light by Home Ec. x Mitzi (@mymitzi)

p. 8: Designed by Diane Rath of The Rath Project (@therathproject), photographed by Erin Kestenbaum (@erinkestenbaum), art is homeowner's own

p. 10 (center): Photographed by Liz Lidgett (@lizlidgettgallery), art by (left to right) Emily Keating Snyder (@EmilyKeatingSnyder), June Street Studio (@JuneStreetStudio), Nate Nettleton (@Nnnnnate)

p. 11 (right): Designed and photographed by Natalie Papier of Home Ec., art by Anne Temple (@annetemplestudio)

p. 12: Designed by Stephanie Theofanos (@moderntraditionsinteriors) and Theodora Miller (@theodoramillerfineart), photographed by Mindie Ballard (@mindieballwell), art above bed by Kevin Sabo (@kevin_sabo), art on shelves by Theodora Miller, Claire McCarty (@bearceramics), Cynthia Erdahl (@cynthiaerdahl), textiles by Theodora Miller

p. 14: Designed by Stephanie Theofanos and Theodora Miller, photographed by Mindie Ballard, art above bed by Kevin Sabo, art on shelves by Theodora Miller, Claire McCarty, Cynthia Erdahl, textiles by Theodora Miller

p. 16 (top): Designed and photographed by Natalie Papier of Home Ec., art by Erik Hoff (@commonorder)

p. 16 (bottom): Designed by Gina Sims Designs, photographed by Cati Teague Photography, art by Veloy Vigil

p. 17 (top): Designed by Natalie Papier of Home Ec., photographed by Megan Easterday of Easterday Creative, art by Garrison Gist (@2gzandcountin)

p. 17 (bottom): Designed and photographed by Natalie Papier of Home Ec., art by Erik Hoff

p. 18: Designed by Natalie Papier of Home Ec., photographed by Margaret Rajic (@margaretrajic), art by Emmanuelle Descraques (@emmanuelle_descraques)

p. 19: Designed and photographed, as well as art, by Angela Chrusciaki Blehm

p. 20: Designed by Gina Sims Designs, photographed by Cati Teague Photography, art by Rocio Navarro (@vanarrocio)

p. 21: Designed by Diane Rath of The Rath Project, photographed by Erin Kestenbaum, art by Angela Chrusciaki Blehm

p. 22: Art by Natalie Osborne (@natalieodecor)

p.23: Designed by Natalie Papier of Home Ec., photographed by Megan Easterday of Easterday Creative

p. 24: © 2023 Haus of Meeshie (@haus_of_meeshie), photographed by Aaron Snyder (@aaronsnyder77), art by Jacqueline Nagel (@jackienagel_art)

p. 27: Designed and photographed by Natalie Papier of Home Ec., art by Mel Remmers (@melremmers)

p. 28: Designed by Gina Sims Designs, photographed by Cati Teague Photography, art is client's own

p. 31: © 2023 Katie Saro (@katiesaro), photographed by Katherine Brooks

p. 32 (top left): Designed by Natalie Papier of Home Ec., photographed by Megan Easterday of Easterday Creative, art by Alexandra Swistak

p. 32 (top right): Designed and photographed by Natalie Papier of Home Ec., art by Malcolm T. Liepke (@malcomtliepke)

p. 32 (bottom left): © 2023 Katie Saro, photographed by Wing Ho, art by Ruth Storc (@light_dark_light)

p. 32 (bottom right): Designed by Diane Rath of The Rath Project, photographed by Erin Kestenbaum, art is vintage

p. 33: Designed by Natalie Papier of Home Ec., photographed by Margaret Rajic, art by Bailey Schmidt (@baileyschmidtart)

p. 34: Designed by Diane Rath of The Rath Project, photographed by Erin Kestenbaum, art (van) by Florent Bodart (@florentbodart), wallpaper by Sanderson

p. 35: Designed by Natalie Papier of Home Ec., photographed by Margaret Rajic, art is vintage Picasso replica from @laircurated, wallpaper by Ottoline (@ottolinedevries)

p. 36: © Flynnside Out, photographed by Robert Peterson (@rusticwhiteinteriors), art by Robert Peterson Photography

p. 38: Designed and photographed by Angela Chrusciaki Blehm, art is vintage

p. 39 (top): Designed and photographed by Kristin Laing (@kristinlaingdesign), art (right) by Evgeniy Monahov (@evgeniymonahov)

p. 39 (bottom): Designed by Rebecca Plumb (@studioplumb), photographed by Nicole Dianne (@nicolediannephoto), art by Studio Plumb

p. 40: Designed and photographed by Natalie Papier of Home Ec., art by Denise Hughes (@denisehughes_art)

p. 41 (top): Designed and photographed by Jewel Marlowe (@jewelmarlowe), art by Theresa Bear (@theresaisabear)

p. 41 (bottom): Designed and photographed by Natalie Papier of Home Ec., art by Emily Ward (@ewardoriginals)

p. 42 (left): Designed and photographed by Jasmine Bible (@jasmine_bible_design), art is vintage

p. 42 (right): Designed and photographed by Natalie Papier of Home Ec., art by Guy Gee (@guygee), wallpaper by Cole & Son (@cole_and_son_wallpapers)

p. 43 (left): Photographed by Natalie Papier of Home Ec., art by Valerie Feo

p. 43 (right): Designed and photographed by Liz Lidgett, art by (left to right) Meghan Bustard (@MeghanBustard), Jenna Brownlee (@JennaBrownlee), Jessi Raulet (@EttaVee)

p. 44: Designed by Natalie Papier of Home Ec., photographed by Megan Easterday of Easterday Creative, portrait of woman with red background and man in hat to her left by Asha (@ashapartyka), all other art is vintage

p. 46: Designed by Natalie Papier of Home Ec., photographed by Megan Easterday of Easterday Creative, portrait of woman with red background and man in hat to her left by Asha, all other art is vintage

p. 47: Designed by Rebecca Plumb, photographed by Studio Plumb, art is vintage

p. 48: Designed by Emily Henderson (@em_henderson), photographed by Sara Ligorria-Tramp (@tramp.studio), art is custom or vintage

p. 50: Designed by Diane Rath of The Rath Project, photographed by Erin Kestenbaum, art is vintage and homeowner's own

p. 51: Designed by Gina Sims Designs, photographed by Abbey Richey (@byabbeysusannephoto), art by Michael Doyle (@michaeldoylestudio)

p. 52: Designed by Gina Sims Designs, photographed by Cati Teague Photography, art is client's own

p. 53 (top): Designed by Stacey-Ann Blake (@designaddictmom), photographed by Kate Rangel (@katerangelphoto), art by Deedee Cheriel (@deedeecheriel), Maggie Stephenson (@_maggiestephenson_), Margo McDaid (@margoinmargate), Poppy Dodge (@poppydodgeart)

p. 53 (bottom): Designed and photographed by Jenasie Earl of Ms Vicious Design (@msviciousdesign), art is vintage

p. 54: Designed by Theodora Miller, photographed by Mindie Ballard, art by Theodora Miller

p. 55: Designed and photographed by Jasmine Bible

p. 56: Designed by Gina Sims Designs, photographed by Cati Teague Photography, art by Susan Hable (@susanhable), Cozamia (@cozamia)

p. 58 (left): Designed and photographed by Natalie Papier of Home Ec., art by Alexandra Tremaine (@atremaine_art)

p. 58 (right): Designed and photographed, as well as art, by Angela Chrusciaki Blehm

p. 59: Designed by Natalie Papier of Home Ec., photographed by Megan Easterday of Easterday Creative, art by Bjørn Wiinblad (@bjornwiinblad)

p. 60: Designed and photographed by Natalie Papier of Home Ec., art by Margo McDaid and Juniper Briggs (@juniperbriggs)

p. 61: © Flynnside Out, photographed by Robert Peterson, art by Gina Julian (@gina_julian), Karen Musgraves (@karenmusgravesartist), Leanne Ford (@leannefordinteriors), Blush and Honey Paper (@blushandhoneypaper), and vintage

p. 62: Designed by Rebecca Plumb, photographed by Geoffrey Bardot (@geoffbardot), art is client's own

p. 63: Designed by Natalie Papier of Home Ec., photographed by Margaret Rajic, art is homeowner's own

p. 64: Designed by Gina Sims Designs, photographed by Cati Teague Photography, mural designed by Gina Sims and painted by Audrey Browning (@abonthewall)

p. 66: Designed by Gina Sims Designs, photographed by Cati Teague Photography, mural by Faye Bell (@fayekaubell), art by Wendover Art Group (@wendoverart), portrait by Peter Robert Keil (@official_peter_keil)

p. 68: Designed by Natalie Papier of Home Ec., photographed by Megan Easterday of Easterday Creative, mural by Buddy Norton and Shelby Lowe of Canned Pineapple Co. (@cannedpineappleco), art by Stacy Kiehl (@stacyk_paints)

p. 69: Designed and photographed by Jasmine Bible, mural by Jasmine Bible, art is vintage

p. 70 (left): Designed and photographed by Racheal Jackson of Banyan Bridges (@banyanbridges), mural by Racheal Jackson

p. 70 (right): Designed and photographed by Natalie Papier of Home Ec., mural by Racheal Jackson

p. 71: Designed and photographed by Racheal Jackson of Banyan Bridges, mural by Racheal and Garrett Jackson (@juxtaphant)

p. 72: Designed by Natalie Papier of Home Ec., photographed by Megan Easterday of Easterday Creative, mural by Racheal Jackson

p. 74: Designed by Natalie Papier of Home Ec., photographed by Megan Easterday of Easterday Creative, mural by Frankie Zombie

p. 75 (top): Designed and photographed by Natalie Papier of Home Ec., mural by Racheal Jackson

p. 75 (bottom): Designed and photographed by Natalie Papier of Home Ec., wallpaper by Etoffe (@etoffe_com), art is vintage reproduction

p. 76: Designed and photographed by Natalie Papier of Home Ec., mural by Liz Kamarul (@liz_kamarul)

p. 78 (left): Designed and photographed by Natalie Papier of Home Ec., mural by @swych19

p. 78 (right): Designed by Jasmine Bible, photographed by Jennifer Morgan Creative (@sandstonecreative), mural by Jasmine Bible

p. 79: Designed and photographed by Natalie Papier of Home Ec., wallpaper by Anthropologie (@anthropologie), art is vintage

p. 80: Designed by Emily Henderson, photographed by Veronica Crawford (@vnrcrawford_), mural by Rebel Walls (@rebelwalls)

p. 81 (left): Designed and photographed by Kristin Laing, mural by Rebel Walls

p. 81 (right): Designed and photographed by Kristin Laing, mural by KEK

p. 82: Designed by Gina Sims Designs, photographed by Cati Teague Photography, mural by Rebel Walls

p. 84: Designed by Diane Rath of The Rath Project, photographed by Erin Kestenbaum, wallpaper by Schumacher (@schumacher1889)

p. 85: Designed by Rebecca Plumb, photographed by Whitney Dianne (@whitneydianne), art by Erica Avila Art (@ericaavilaart), wallpaper by Milton & King (@miltonandking)

p. 86 (left): Designed and photographed by Jenasie Earl, Ms Vicious Design, wallpaper by Milton & King

p. 86 (right): Designed by Natalie Papier of Home Ec., photographed by Megan Easterday of Easterday Creative, art by Alexandra Swistak, wallpaper by Belarte Studio (@belartestudio)

p. 87: Designed and photographed by Natalie Papier of Home Ec., plates by Margo McDaid, portrait by Asha

p. 88: Designed by Natalie Papier of Home Ec., photographed by Megan Easterday of Easterday Creative, wallpaper by Hygge & West (@hyggeandwest)

p. 89: Designed and photographed by Jewel Marlowe, art is vintage, wallpaper by Spoonflower (@spoonflower)

p. 90: Rendering by Mitchell Black (@mitchell_black)

p. 91: Designed by Diane Rath of The Rath Project, photographed by Erin Kestenbaum, wallpaper by York Wallcoverings (@york_wallcoverings)

p. 92: Designed by Natalie Papier of Home Ec., photographed by Megan Easterday of Easterday Creative, art is vintage

p. 95: Designed and photographed by Natalie Papier of Home Ec., piano by Frankie Zombie

p. 96: Designed by Diane Rath of The Rath Project, photographed by Erin Kestenbaum, art is vintage

p. 97: Designed by Jess Bunge (@jessbunge), photographed by Sara Ligorria-Tramp, wooden art by Katie Gong (@katie.gong)

p. 98 (top left): Designed and photographed by Natalie Papier of Home Ec.

p. 98 (top right): Designed and photographed by Natalie Papier of Home Ec., art by Daniel Freaker (@freakerstudio), Joe Kameen (@joekameen), Lumas Gallery (@lumas_gallery), Michael Hedges (@michaelhedgesart), Scully & Scully (@scullyandscully), Stray Dog Designs (@straydogdesigns)

p. 98 (bottom left): Designed and photographed, as well as ribbon art, by Angela Chrusciaki Blehm, other art by Juliet Blehm, Hayley Mitchell, Martin Summers

p. 98 (bottom right): Designed and photographed by Natalie Papier of Home Ec., art by Margo McDaid and Juniper Briggs

p. 99: Designed by Natalie Papier of Home Ec., photographed by Megan Easterday of Easterday Creative, light by Home Ec. x Mitzi

p. 100: Designed by Jasmine Bible, photographed by Jennifer Morgan Creative, fiber art by Jasmine Bible

p. 102: Designed by Natalie Papier of Home Ec., photographed by Megan Easterday of Easterday Creative, art by Brooks Burns (@brooksburns_art), light by Home Ec. x Mitzi

p. 103: Designed by Natalie Papier of Home Ec., photographed by Megan Easterday of Easterday Creative, art by Guzzo Pinc (@guzzopinc), light by Home Ec. x Mitzi, sculptural trees by House of Nomad (@houseofnomaddesign)

p. 104 (left): Designed and photographed, as well as art, by Angela Chrusciaki Blehm

p. 104 (center): Designed by Natalie Papier of Home Ec., photographed by Megan Easterday of Easterday Creative, art by Frankie Zombie

p. 104 (fold): Photographed by Natalie Papier of Home Ec., art by Herb Williams (@herbwilliamsart)

p. 105: Designed and photographed by Natalie Papier of Home Ec., pillows by Gwen Rucker (@happygwensday)

p. 106: © Flynnside Out, photographed by Robert Peterson

p. 107: Designed by Emily Henderson, photographed by Kaitlin Green (@kaitlinmgreen_photo), art is vintage

p. 108: Designed by Rebecca Plumb, photographed by Geoffrey Bardot, art by Artfully Walls (@artfullywalls), hand-painted oars by Lisa Bardot (@lisabardot)

p. 110: Designed and photographed by Natalie Papier of Home Ec., art by Erin Cone (@erinconestudio) via Lumas Gallery

p. 111: Designed by Natalie Papier of Home Ec., photographed by Megan Easterday of Easterday Creative, tile by Fireclay (@fireclaytile)

p. 112: Designed by Elsie Larson (@elsielarson), photographed by Amber Bentley (@amber_m_bentley)

p. 114: Designed by Elsie Larson, photographed by Amber Bentley

p. 115: Designed by Natalie Papier of Home Ec., photographed by Megan Easterday of Easterday Creative, sculpture on left by The Frenchman's Wife (@thefrenchmanswife) and vintage

p. 117: Designed by Diane Rath of The Rath Project, photographed by Erin Kestenbaum, wallpaper by Spoonflower

p. 118: Designed and photographed by Natalie Papier of Home Ec.

p. 119: Designed and photographed by Natalie Papier of Home Ec.

p. 120: Designed and photographed by Natalie Papier of Home Ec., art by Jennifer Lawrence (@jenniferlawrencephoto)

p. 121 (top): Designed and photographed by Natalie Papier of Home Ec., art by Garrison Gist, Yellowpop (@yellowpop)

p. 121 (bottom): Designed and photographed by Natalie Papier of Home Ec., art by Yellowpop

p. 122 (left): © 2023 Cathy M. LeVitre (@cathymlevitre)

p. 122 (right): Designed by Natalie Papier of Home Ec., photographed by Megan Easterday of Easterday Creative, piano by Frankie Zombie, light by Home Ec. x Mitzi

p. 123: Designed and photographed by Natalie Papier of Home Ec., art by Natalie Osborne

p. 124: Designed and photographed by Haneen Matt (@haneens_haven), art from Etsy

p. 125 (top): Designed by Gina Sims Designs, photographed by Cati Teague Photography, wallpaper by Schumacher (@shumacher1889), art is vintage

p. 125 (bottom): Designed by Gina Sims Designs, photographed by Cati Teague Photography, art by James Dean (@jamesdeanart), Rebecca Cristante (@rebeccacristante), Robert Lee (@methanestudios), Bitter Southerner (@bittersoutherner), Meagan Berardi (@meganhop)

p. 126: Designed and photographed by Natalie Papier of Home Ec., art is vintage

p. 129 (top left): © Flynnside Out, photographed by Robert Peterson, art is vintage

p. 129 (top right): Photographed by Farron Feiner (@farronfeiner), weaving by Farron Feiner

p. 129 (bottom left): Designed and photographed by Natalie Papier of Home Ec., portrait by Guy Gee

p. 129 (bottom right): © Flynnside Out, photographed by Robert Peterson, art by Nathalie Carrigan (@wooltimber)

p. 130: Designed by Gina Sims Designs, photographed by Cati Teague Photography

p. 132: © 2023 Katie Saro, photographed by Katie Sarokhanian

p. 133: Designed by Natalie Papier of Home Ec., photographed by Megan Easterday of Easterday Creative, art by Peter Keil

p. 134: Designed by Natalie Papier of Home Ec., photographed by Megan Easterday of Easterday Creative, art is vintage

p. 135: Designed by Natalie Papier of Home Ec., photographed by Megan Easterday of Easterday Creative, light by Home Ec. x Mitzi

p. 136: Designed by Emily Henderson, photographed by Sara Ligorria-Tramp, art is custom

p. 137 (top left): Designed and photographed by Amara Hasham (@thepajaamahub)

p. 137 (top right): Designed and photographed by Evie Kemp (@eviekemp), art by Victoria Topping (@victoriatoppingstudio), Evie Kemp

p. 137 (bottom left): Designed and photographed by Amara Hasham

p. 137 (bottom right): Designed and photographed by Kate Pearce (@katepearcevintage)

p. 139: Designed and photographed by Natalie Papier of Home Ec., art by Minted (@minted) and Margo McDaid

p. 140: Designed by Stephan Eicker (@eickerdesign), photography © James McDonald (@james_mcdonald _photography), art by Knut Rumohr

p. 144: Designed and photographed by Natalie Papier of Home Ec., art by Erik Hoff and thrifted

p. 145 (top): Designed and photographed, as well as art and mural, by Angela Chrusciaki Blehm

p. 145 (bottom): Designed by Natalie Papier of Home Ec., photographed by Margaret Rajic, art is homeowner's own

p. 146: Designed by Gina Sims Designs, photographed by Cati Teague Photography, wallpaper by A-Street Prints (@astreetprints), art by Christopher Kennedy (@christopherkennedyinc) and Dorothy Forrest

p. 149: Designed by Jasmine Bible, photographed by Jennifer Morgan Creative, faux burl wood table by Jasmine Bible

p. 150 (top): Designed and photographed by Natalie Papier of Home Ec., art by Tishk Barzanji (@tishkbarzanji) and Art.com (@artdotcom)

p. 150 (bottom): Designed by Danielle McKim (@tuftinteriors), photographed by Elizabeth Larson Photography (@elizabethlarsonphotography), art prints from Etsy

p. 151 (top): Designed and photographed by Shawna Freeman (@bellybaila), art is vintage

p. 151 (bottom): © 2023 Katie Saro, photographed by Katie Sarokhanian

p. 152 (top): Designed by Diane Rath of The Rath Project, photographed by Erin Kestenbaum

p. 152 (bottom): Designed by Rebecca Plumb, photographed by Camp Golden Bear (@campgoldenbear), art by Cliff McCurdy

p. 153 (top): Designed by Natalie Papier of Home Ec., photographed by Christopher Testani (@christophertestani), art by Guzzo Pinc

p. 153 (bottom): Designed by Diane Rath of The Rath Project, photographed by Erin Kestenbaum

p. 154 (top): Designed by Natalie Papier of Home Ec., photographed by Megan Easterday of Easterday Creative, mural by Racheal Jackson, art by Frankie Zombie

p. 154 (bottom): Designed and photographed by Liz Kamarul, art by Christina Flowers (@hellochristinaflowers)

p. 155 (top): Designed and photographed by Kate Pearce

p. 155 (bottom): Designed by Jasmine Bible, photographed by Jennifer Morgan Creative, floor mural by Jasmine Bible

p. 156 (top): Designed by Diane Rath of The Rath Project, photographed by Erin Kestenbaum, art is vintage

p. 156 (bottom): © 2023 Katie Saro, photographed by and art by Katie Sarokhanian

p. 157 (top): Designed by Stacey-Ann Blake, photographed by Kate Rangel, art by Keely Reyes (@krco_creative)

p. 157 (bottom): Designed by Jasmine Bible, photographed by Jennifer Morgan Creative, ceiling mural by Jasmine Bible

p. 158 (top): Designed and photographed, as well as art, by Rosie Case (@rosie.case)

p. 158 (bottom): Designed by Diane Rath of The Rath Project, photographed by Erin Kestenbaum, art is vintage and homeowner's own

p. 159 (top): © 2023 Katie Saro, photographed by Katie Sarokhanian, art by Katie Sarokhanian and her kids

p. 159 (bottom): © 2023 Katie Saro, photographed by Katie Sarokhanian, art by Charlie Sisson

p. 160 (left): Designed and photographed by Natalie Papier of Home Ec., art by Tishk Barzanji

p. 160 (right): Designed by Jasmine Bible, photographed by Jennifer Morgan Creative, mural by Jasmine Bible

p. 161 (left): Designed by Diane Rath of The Rath Project, photographed by Erin Kestenbaum, art is vintage or thrifted

p. 161 (right): Designed by Diane Rath of The Rath Project, photographed by Erin Kestenbaum, art is vintage

p. 162: Designed by Diane Rath of The Rath Project, photographed by Erin Kestenbaum

p. 163: Designed and photographed by Natalie Papier of Home Ec.

p. 164: Designed by Natalie Papier of Home Ec., photographed by Megan Easterday of Easterday Creative, art by Frances Berry Moreno (@where_is_frances), light by Home Ec. x Mitzi

p. 166: Designed by Gina Sims Designs, photographed by Cati Teague Photography, wallpaper by Wallpaper Direct (@wallpaperdirect)

p. 168: Designed by Diane Rath of The Rath Project, photographed by Erin Kestenbaum, art is client's own

p. 169 (left): © Flynnside Out, photographed by Robert Peterson, art by Robert Peterson Photography, Chris Burkard (@chrisburkard)

p. 169 (right): Designed by Diane Rath of The Rath Project, photographed by Erin Kestenbaum, art by Evan Hecox (@evanhecox)

p. 170: Designed by Natalie Papier of Home Ec., photographed by Margaret Rajic, art by Juniper Briggs

p. 171: Designed and photographed by Jewel Marlowe, art is vintage

p. 172: Designed and photographed by Natalie Papier of Home Ec., mural by Racheal Jackson

p. 173: Designed and photographed, as well as mural, by Natalie Papier of Home Ec.

p. 174: Designed and photographed by Natalie Papier of Home Ec., art by Kathi Graves (@kathigravesart), wallpaper from Etsy

p. 175: Designed and photographed by Natalie Papier of Home Ec., portrait by Asha, all other art is vintage

p. 176: Designed and photographed by Rosie Case, vintage art by Max Mata

p. 177: Designed by Natalie Papier of Home Ec., photographed by Margaret Rajic

p. 178: © Flynnside Out, photographed by Robert Peterson

p. 179: Designed by Natalie Papier of Home Ec., photographed by Tiffany Ashmore of Kinston Photography (@kinstonphotography)

p. 180: Designed and photographed by Kate Pearce, wallpaper by Belarte Studio

p. 181: Designed and photographed by Natalie Papier of Home Ec., wallpaper by House of Nomad

p. 182: Designed by Natalie Papier of Home Ec., photographed by Megan Easterday of Easterday Creative

p. 184: Designed by Natalie Papier of Home Ec., photographed by Megan Easterday of Easterday Creative

p. 186 (left): Designed by Rebecca Plumb, photographed by Nicole Dianne, art by Erica Avila

p. 186 (right): Designed by Gina Sims Designs, photographed by Cati Teague Photography, art by Susan Hable, Janet Hill Studio (@janethillstudio)

p. 187: Designed by Diane Rath of The Rath Project, photographed by Rebecca Stern (@rebeccasternart), art is vintage from Etsy, wallpaper by World of Wallpaper (@worldofwallpaperuk)

p. 188: Designed by Rebecca Plumb, photographed by Studio Plumb, art by Sarah Golden (@sarahgoldenart), wallpaper by Milton & King

p. 190: Designed by Rebecca Plumb, photographed by Studio Plumb, art is vintage

p. 191: Designed by Gina Sims Designs, photographed by Cati Teague Photography, art by Bongo Printables

p. 193: Designed by Diane Rath of The Rath Project, photographed by Erin Kestenbaum

p. 194: Designed by Natalie Papier of Home Ec., photographed by Megan Easterday of Easterday Creative, art is vintage

p. 195: © Flynnside Out, photographed by Robert Peterson

p. 196: Designed by Rebecca Plumb, photographed by Studio Plumb, art by Kelly O'Neal (@officialkellyoneal) for Leftbank Art (@leftbankart)

p. 197: Designed and photographed by Natalie Papier of Home Ec.

p. 198: © 2023 Haus of Meeshie, photographed by Aaron Snyder, art by Jacqueline Nagel

p. 200 (left): Designed by Natalie Papier of Home Ec., photographed by Megan Easterday of Easterday Creative, light by Home Ec. x Mitzi

p. 200 (right): Designed by Natalie Papier of Home Ec., photographed by Megan Easterday of Easterday Creative, light

by Home Ec. x Mitzi, vintage burlwood modular piece from Slate Interiors (@slateinteriors)

p. 201: Designed by Natalie Papier of Home Ec., photographed by Megan Easterday of Easterday Creative, light by Home Ec. x Mitzi

p. 203: Designed by Natalie Papier of Home Ec., photographed by Megan Easterday of Easterday Creative, art by Bailey Schmidt and Daniel Freaker, shelving by Ferney Mercado (@chard.nc)

p. 204: Designed by Elsie Larson, photographed by Amber Bentley

p. 205: Designed and photographed by Racheal Jackson of Banyan Bridges, mural by Racheal Jackson

p. 206: Designed by Gina Sims Designs, photographed by Cati Teague Photography, wallpaper by Hygge & West

p. 207: Designed by Diane Rath of The Rath Project, photographed by Erin Kestenbaum, wallpaper by NuWallpaper by Wall Pops (@wallpops)

p. 208: Designed by Rebecca Plumb, photographed by Nicole Dianne, art by Studio Plumb, wallpaper by Milton & King

p. 209 (left): Designed and photographed by Natalie Papier of Home Ec., art is vintage

p. 209 (right): Designed and photographed by Kate Pearce, wallpaper by Belarte Studio

p. 210: Designed by Rebecca Plumb, photographed by Studio Plumb, art by Kelly O'Neal for Leftbank Art

p. 212: Designed by Diane Rath of The Rath Project, photographed by Erin Kestenbaum, art is vintage

p. 213: Designed and photographed by Natalie Papier of Home Ec., art by Mel Remmers

p. 214: Photographed by and art by Carrie Gillen (@carriegillenstl)

p. 215: Designed by Natalie Papier of Home Ec., photographed by Megan Easterday of Easterday Creative, light by Home Ec. x Mitzi

p. 216 (left): Designed by Diane Rath of The Rath Project, photographed by Erin Kestenbaum, art is homeowner's own, wallpaper by Divine Savages (@divinesavages)

p. 216 (fold): Designed by Diane Rath of The Rath Project, photographed by Erin Kestenbaum, art by Katy Garry (@katygarryfineart)

p. 217 (right): Designed by Natalie Papier of Home Ec., photographed by Megan Easterday of Easterday Creative, art by Faith Christiansen Smeets (@faithchristiansensmeets)

p. 218 (left): Designed and photographed by Amara Hasham

p. 218 (right): Designed and photographed by Kate Pearce, art by Tauba Auerbach (@tau_au)

p. 219: Designed by Natalie Papier of Home Ec. and Kelsey Diane Design, photographed by Megan Easterday of Easterday Creative, wallpaper by Belarte Studio, art is vintage from Etsy

p. 220: Designed by Gina Sims Designs, photographed by Cati Teague Photography, art by Wendover Art Group

p. 221: Designed and photographed by Kate Pearce

p. 222: © Flynnside Out, photographed by Robert Peterson, art by Robert Peterson Photography

p. 223: Designed and photographed by Natalie Papier of Home Ec.

p. 224: Designed by Diane Rath of The Rath Project, photographed by Erin Kestenbaum

p. 225: © 2023 Cathy M. LeVitre

p. 226: Designed by Diane Rath of The Rath Project, photographed by Rebecca Stern

p. 227: Designed by Natalie Papier of Home Ec., photographed by Megan Easterday of Easterday Creative, mural by Fine & Dandy Co. (@fineanddandyco), light by Lightology (@lightology)

p. 228: Designed by Natalie Papier of Home Ec., photographed by Megan Easterday of Easterday Creative, art is vintage, light by Home Ec. x Mitzi

p. 229: Designed and photographed by Natalie Papier of Home Ec., art by Frankie Zombie

p. 230: Designed by Natalie Papier of Home Ec., photographed by Megan Easterday of Easterday Creative

p. 232: Designed and photographed by Natalie Papier of Home Ec.

p. 234: Designed by Orla Read Design Studio (@orlaread), photographed by Darren Chung

p. 235 (top): Designed by Kimille Taylor (@kimilletaylor), photograph by Jason Schmidt (@jasonschmidtstudio), art by Grace Weaver (@weaver_grace)

p. 235 (bottom): Designed and photographed by Lacy Hoysradt (@livingawilderlife), art by Daniel Götesson (@ektaektaekta) in collaboration with Fine Little Day (@finelittleday)

p. 236: Designed by Natalie Papier of Home Ec., photographed by Megan Easterday of Easterday Creative, mural by Fine & Dandy Co., light by Home Ec. x Mitzi

p. 238: Designed by Rebecca Plumb, photographed by Nicole Dianne, art by Erica Avila, Studio Plumb

p. 240: Designed and photographed by Natalie Papier of Home Ec., art is client's own

p. 241: Designed by Diane Rath of The Rath Project, photographed by Erin Kestenbaum, art is an antique from The Collective (@thecollectivect), wallpaper by Cole & Son

p. 242: Designed by Gina Sims Designs, photographed by Cati Teague Photography, wallpaper by A-Street Prints

p. 244: Designed by Diane Rath of The Rath Project, photographed by Erin Kestenbaum, wallpaper by Art Wall Collection (@artwallcollection)

p. 245: Designed by Diane Rath of The Rath Project, photographed by Erin Kestenbaum, art by Chagall from homeowner's collection

p. 246: Designed by Natalie Papier of Home Ec., photographed by Tiffany Ashmore of Kinston Photography

p. 248 (top left): Designed and photographed by Natalie Papier of Home Ec., art by Rachael Van Dyke (@vandyker)

p. 248 (top right): Designed and photographed by Natalie Papier of Home Ec., art by Golsa Golchini (@golsa.golchini)

p. 248 (bottom left): Designed and photographed by Natalie Papier of Home Ec., art by Carrie Gillen

p. 248 (bottom right): Designed and photographed by Natalie Papier of Home Ec., art by Brittany Smith (@brittanysmithstudio)

p. 258: Designed by Diane Rath of The Rath Project, photographed by Rebecca Stern, art by Jessica Poundstone (@jessicapoundstone) via Chairish (@chairishco)

p. 260 (left): Photographed by Amanda Anderson (@amandaandersonphotography)

p. 260 (right): Photographed by Samantha Lowe (@samantha_lowe_)

acknowledgments

This book has been a labor of love for more than two years and took a mountain of people beyond the two of us to bring it to life. Thank you to *Real Simple* magazine for connecting us; our agent, Kristin van Ogtrop, for suggesting the partnership; the team at Voracious for seeing the potential in our art-forward approach; and Danielle Claro for editing our ideas with such skill and grace. Thanks to all of the artists, designers, and photographers who shared their incredible work with us and continue to inspire and delight. — N.P. & S.S.

To my dad, Kelly Hass, who first introduced me to the beauty of art and home craftsmanship: your passion for what a home is and the potential that each one holds has become the backbone of my career. Thanks to Francie Scoflanc, my childhood YMCA art teacher, who kicked off my art obsession. Thank you to Megan Easterday, photographer extraordinaire, who helps me let loose and captures the light within every space.

Alan, Kellen, and Maddie: how lucky I am to have my own little family as my cheerleaders through all of this. Thank you for your unconditional love, support, and patience — even when I decide to repaint another room in our house . . . again.

To my Instagram community: your endless inspiration, unwavering support, and genuine friendships have made my career what it is today — truly proving that this is a community and not a competition.

A huge thank-you to my incredible friends, who have continued to bolster my confidence in the creation of this brand-new career — from coming up with a name for my business (thank you, Oak Park Book Club ladies) to being steady pillars when I needed you most. You know who you are.

The biggest thank-you of all to my clients (many of whom have become true friends of mine) for your trust, enthusiasm, and generally just keeping this girl in business . . .

To Stephanie Sisco, the most organized, consistent, dedicated writer of all: there would be no book if not for you making sense out of all my nonsense. — N.P.

Immense gratitude to Danielle Claro. You have been my mentor and my champion since the start of my career, and you helped take this book to the next level. I am lucky to call you my friend.

To my husband, Peter Luccarelli, thank you for your unwavering support (and for recognizing the dominance of the Oxford comma). P.J. and Will, you are my joy. Julie Sisco, none of this could have been done without you. Inconceivable. Right, Dale Sisco?

Finally, Natalie, thank you for infusing color into this world. Your passion is infectious, and I am so glad to be in your orbit. — S.S.

About the authors

Natalie Papier is a designer, art curator, and TV personality based in Charlotte, North Carolina, who believes that meaningful design starts with the art. Papier is a champion for artists across the globe and regularly features her current favorites on her Instagram account (@home_ec_op) and her Magnolia Network show, *Artfully Designed*. Additionally, she has a handful of product partnerships, from a lighting line with Mitzi to a wallpaper collection with Mitchell Black.

   Along with her husband, Alan, and kids, Kellen and Maddie, Natalie moved from Chicago to Charlotte in 2020 (with dog, Billy, and cat, Boots, in tow) and brought her design firm, Home Ec., and a whole lot of color along with her.

Stephanie Sisco is a writer based in Tampa, Florida. She and Papier met when Sisco was the home director at *Real Simple* magazine in New York City. After giving birth to her first son, P.J., Sisco and her family moved home to Florida, and she and Papier reconnected to develop a book proposal. Sisco has welcomed another son, William, while working with Papier on this book.

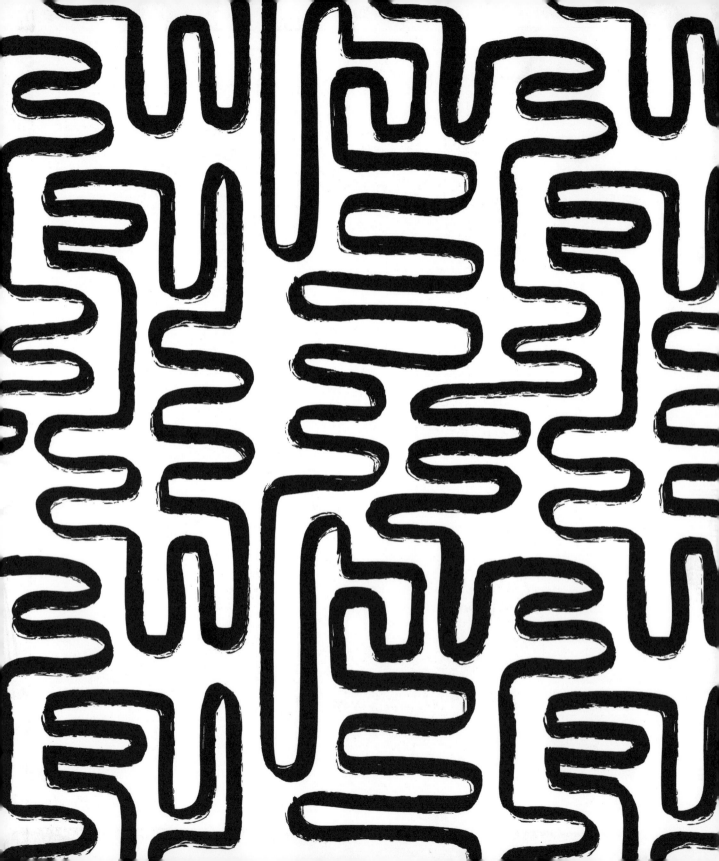